SELECTED POEMS

Contents

Acknowledgments

The publication of this volume has been made possible by the generous help and concern of a number of people, to whom thanks are due. First of all to Lola Szladits, the late Curator of the Berg Collection of the New York Public Library, whose interest in Jean Garrigue's work led to the establishment of the archive of her manuscripts in the Berg Collection. From the beginning, Dr. Szladits's encouragement of the project to publish this volume was invaluable. Bonne August, with the help of Brian McInerney of the Berg Collection, ordered and cataloged the archive and traced a number of uncollected and unpublished poems. Lee Upton made helpful suggestions and with Bonne August participated in the selection of poems for this volume. Claire Gleitman transcribed the manuscript and assisted in the proofreading of the text.

A special debt of gratitude is owed to J. D. McClatchy for writing the Introduction and providing constructive advice in the process of publication.

Most gratitude of all is due to Leslie Katz, who first conceived of this book and worked continuously to bring it to fruition, and to the Eakins Press Foundation, whose contribution finally enabled it to be published in its present form.

Aileen Ward
Executrix of the
Estate of Jean Garrigue

Introduction

"On Monday," Delmore Schwartz wrote, "I sent some of your poems, hurriedly and perhaps poorly chosen, to Laughlin." Schwartz's letter to Jean Garrigue, dated August 1, 1942, was meant to encourage her. As teacher and student, they had met that summer at the Cummington School of the Arts, and Garrigue had been depressed. Marianne Moore, with whom Garrigue also worked that summer in the Berkshires, noticed the young poet's uncertainties and discontents, and by praising the well-knit vigilance and experienced tone of her work Moore may have been indirectly urging Garrigue to cultivate those same qualities in her life. Some of Garrigue's self-doubts were temperamental, and shadowed her whole career. Some were any beginner's wooziness in the face of daunting traditions and possibilities. Over the years Garrigue managed to dispel those doubts, most often by making them into art. Her confidence—what Robert Lowell once called her "big sweep and untiring deftness"—cost. But over and over she found new ways to control her experience and refresh her art. Ten years after first meeting Garrigue, Moore was astonished by the power of her poems and by the capacity of her feelings both to resist and accept. Twenty years later another phrase of Moore's, from one of her last letters to Garrigue, remains the best description of the resolve, the drama, the achievement of Garrigue's work. You've shown, wrote Moore, an "unexampled heroism."

But none of this was evident at the start. "I know that you are a good poet," Schwartz's letter continues, "and perhaps to be a very good one and this makes me think, How sad that you should waste time and emotion on self-doubt. How might you be persuaded that I mean and perhaps know what I say about the goodness of your poems?" To become a Very Good Poet had been Garrigue's life-long ambition. When they were young, her sister asked her what she most wanted in life. "Fame as a writer," she answered. Her sister has also recalled Garrigue as "an impatient and fretful little child," only soothed by music; and as a rebellious student, expelled from school for bad behavior, but spending hours in her third-floor room at home reading Shelley, Keats, Swinburne, the Imagists, and H.D.—who, she once said, "made daring to write poetry seem possible." She went to hear Edna St. Vincent Millay read, and excitedly spent all her savings—twenty-five dollars—on a first edition of Millay's poems.

Garrigue was born in Evansville, Indiana, on December 8, 1912 (though the date she gave later was 1914). Raised in Indianapolis and educated at the Universities of Chicago (where her roommate was Marguerite Young) and Iowa, she had a midwesterner's yearning for the cultural blandishments and social freedoms of the East. She visited Paris as soon as possible, and when she first arrived to live in New York City, she changed her name from the demure Gertrude Louise Garrigus to the more poetic Jean Garrigue. (The sexual ambiguity of her first name may be noted, and the version of her surname brings it closer to its proper French spelling, Garrigues, a Huguenot family name from the Languedoc. Originally, the name was Garric, meaning "oak." The English actor David Garrick was from the same family.) It was in New York in 1940, she later recalled, "that I felt myself delivered and as it were in possession of a tongue. All dates from that, despite a lost trunkful of the proverbial journals, notes, poems and prose—that trail of attempts and explorations the writer must blaze."

The Kenyon Review first published a group of Garrigue's poems in 1941, and she began to contribute stories and reviews to the magazine as well. There were other small successes and frustrations in those early years. To pay her way she worked as a research editor at *Collier's*, then edited a monthly information sheet for the USO, and finally—these were the war years—ended up as assistant editor of an aeronautical magazine, *The Flying Cadet*. None of this was evident, though, in the lush romantic poems she was writing in her off-hours. Marianne Moore told her, "You have all you need," but wished she would deal with more homely subjects and abandon her "esthetic obsession with sex." And Schwartz noted what from the very beginning were Garrigue's immortal longings, her metaphysical drive toward excess and paradox, toward the abstract and unknown. "Gautier said that critics became too complicated when they discussed his poetry," Schwartz wrote to her. " 'I am merely one for whom the visible world exists.' So you should say, 'I am really one for whom the invisible world exists; but the visible also.' "

The publisher and poet James Laughlin remembers Delmore Schwartz's enthusiastic letter; he remembers too his first meeting with Garrigue: "Jean turned out to be very much the *jeune fille bien élevée,* as pure as she was pristine. No matter, I found Delmore quite right." In 1944 he included her work in the third series of his annual New Directions collection, *Five Young American Poets,* along with debuts by John Frederick Nims and Tennessee Williams. Laughlin goes on to write:

> It's hard to remember how I felt about Jean's poetry forty years ago, so much that she did quickly became part of a general tradition, for she was much imitated. What seized me at once was that she didn't sound like all the others. And it was refreshing to come on a young poet who could be both intellectual and personal in the same poem. She had, I felt then, a sure sense for the visual, and she had a fine ear for putting words together. I doubt if anyone ever compared her to Ovid but she had some of his, or the English equivalent of his smoothness of phrasing. There is a lovely delicacy about so many of the poems, but they don't get soft. There are always bones under the flesh. The freshness, always the freshness comes back to me. She was a joy to publish. I never had to suggest changes. The poems were themselves and they were right.

The bluntly titled *Thirty-six Poems and a Few Songs*—Garrigue's name for her share of *Five Young American Poets*—has just thirty-six poems in the collection, so her title is meant slyly to stress the implicit lyric character of all the work. In a brief preface, Garrigue declares her devotion less to the example of the English metaphysical poets than to T. S. Eliot's widely influential version of their strengths. She praises—and thereby asks the reader to notice in her own poems—a style that jostles its quartz-sides and lengthens its perspectives with irony, that "allows gracious license to the fluctuations, recoils and most delicate expeditions into the matter of the subject." Poetic "truth" rests in relationships, and it is the poet's task to describe and to connect. If his subject is, say, a hill, then "he wants all of the hill that is useful, that is, to his poem: its roughness or its glabrous surface, its rocks or peaked loaf, its nubile or spartan look: but he also wants to interpret, that is, to humanize, to bring it into the realm of his, the poet's, into conjunction with railroad ties or sunflowers, lighthouses or Love or God."

These early poems by Garrigue, with their pulsing rhythms, lightly brushed-in rhymes, and elaborately worked conceits are very much in the high style of the day—that day being the time of the New Critics, who insisted that a poem represented an action, that its dramatic effects were extensions of its voice, that it unfolded its meanings not with any discursive logic but in an expressive complex of images. Poems of this period most nearly resembled the creative mind itself: sedulous, self-reflective, allusively cultured, with an aloof integrity and an evident, though not necessarily apparent, continuity between their manifold surfaces and their unconscious depths or motives. From the start, though, Garrigue's voice sounded strange. She tried for a "poetic diction" that could speak of feelings glimpsed beneath her thought-provoking designs, that could explore "our landscape of love . . . [a] rich and violent country." Romantic and symbolist motifs—moon and mirror, dark wood and golden hair—abound. But the lapidary eloquence of her textures wants continually to give way. Underneath the brook's face is, skull-like, "a building made by shadow." Beyond the restraining glassen surfaces is "the improvident flood." It is this tension that gives her poems their force, their compelling restlessness.

> Leaping and leaping our hearts,
> Sight staggered; if landscape was
> Different than we, so were we,
> So were we, falling, ourselves from
> Ourselves cut off, emblem of love
> Torn in two.

When he was in prep school, John Ashbery now recalls, he read these first poems by Garrigue with a thrilled eagerness. There was "a surreal, dream-like quality" to them that he later found only in French poetry, and "a strangeness that I sympathized with." Both *The*

Ego and the Centaur (1947) and *The Monument Rose* (1953) con-
tinue the baroque anxieties, the extravagant rhetorical gestures, the
estranging sympathies of Garrigue's first book. The poems are divina-
tions and spells. States of being are conjured. Language is translated
into experience. To be sure, one hears occasional echoes in that lan-
guage. Here is Auden (while at Cummington, Garrigue appeared in a
production of *The Ascent of F-6*):

> The time for thinking is useless,
> The time for acting is done;
> It seems in this noisy city
> Girded by tracks and by rivers
> Not even the sky is natural
> With it supple, escaping clouds.

And here Eliot:

> In the garden the roses scattered
> When under the wickets I came
> To their blooming there on the mound.

This could be Hart Crane or Dylan Thomas:

> O nuptial drug and condiment of rite,
> O tempter to an inwardness of sight,
> Dwarfs, indigo, within whose opera,
> O bridal jest, you circummortal us,
> Nuptial of vacancy who wizards us.

Garrigue first read Dylan Thomas in *Poetry* in 1938 and was
struck by "the shock and dazzle and extraordinary newness of his
language, concept and organization. . . . He skirts meaning, walks
around it and above it." In his turn, Thomas later called her "a deeply
serious poet with a fine ear and a lovely, dangerous voice of her own."
In her first three books, Garrigue conceived her own ambition, her
own *voice*, in a manner not unlike Thomas's. She cared not for the
beat of the line but for the cadence of the sentence, charged with
emotion. She wanted what Coleridge called "the figured language

of thought," a rapturous cascade of metaphor, and a transfiguring moral energy. Above all she wanted a new language for poetry: explosive, spellbound, profusive. But the language was to be both scrim and scalpel; she was continually impatient to push words past their easy referential duties, to use language not to recount but to create experience. Among her papers, she left this undated note:

> It is the poet's faith that there is reality, if not realities upon realities back of, behind, beyond the enchanting surfaces and appearances of "reality." Perhaps his most strenuous occupation is to peel himself, to divest himself, to bare himself of the evil enchantments that "surface reality" man cast upon him in order that he may strip himself down to that level of seeing and feeling whereby his reality may be able to meet the reality within and behind what is seen and known to the senses.

In the 1950s Garrigue began to teach. First at Bard, later at Queens, the New School, the University of Connecticut, and at Smith, she taught poetry courses. One of her students at Bard, the poet Grace Schulman, remembers her "affection for and devotion to her students—not a hovering maternal affection but a deep respect for their vocation and their hopes." It was during this period too that her poems entered a new phase—one, ironically, less studied than her early work. Her ambition had matured, and her poems, if less intense, became more poised and complex. "A Figure for J. V. Meer," at once an homage to Vermeer and an emblematic self-portrait, views the objects in the world, the *given,* as "Signs for the ungiven thing / She converses with on that light gathering in." In Vermeer's paintings, the glistening seed pearls scattered everywhere are meant by the artist both to reflect light and to create it within the picture's frame. So too Garrigue's heightened rhetorical deployment of details. Each rose or drop of blood is an atomy of passion, each a translucence, "Like a clarity of being become / A concordance, an equation, this light / With the soul transformed in its chamber." A clarity that balances and transforms is the hallmark of Garrigue's middle period.

Each book now is anchored by a long poem: "For the Fountains and Fountaineers of Villa d'Este," "Pays Perdu," "The Grand

Canyon," "Studies for an Actress." She once said, "I prefer elaborate structures to functional slick ones. Chopin, Keats, and Proust were early powerful influences. So were mountains and water." For her, art was as "real" as nature, Proust as natural as a mountain, as elemental as water. Art, in fact, was a magical way for her to enter into the natural world. To gaze at the fountains of the Villa d'Este long enough to see through their exquisite artificiality was to become transfigured, to return to a natural state in a manner entirely mythological:

> I am dense as lichen,
> Primordial as fern,
> Or, like that tree split at its base,
> Covert for winter creatures and water-retreated life,
> Tip with my boughs very serpent green,
> Or in a grand spirit of play
> Spurt water out of my nostrils.

A gloss on this poem's "elaborate structure," and on her aesthetic in general, may properly be found in her essay on Chartres. To enter this or the other long Garrigue poems is like her own impression of entering the great Gothic cathedral: "the length and the height, the confined vastity, the determined obscurity clarified by windows of burning light." To contemplate the whole is to wonder "by what vigorous rationalism and dense pounds of masonry an interior all spirit is kept contained."

"Pays Perdu" is a ramble, a diaristic account that draws on Garrigue's strengths as a novelist. Set in Keats's imagined Provençe, the poem is itself a landscape, with stretches of verse interspersed with heaped-up prose. Relaxed and intimate, its tone and control are a measure of the authority of Garrigue's style in these middle years. Her favorite subjects were travel (almost always a voyage inward as well) and love (usually toured as a foreign place). Love—bad love, wronged love, futile or wrecked love—was her counterpart to imagination. What she lost in life—in a passionate life, fraught with affairs with both sexes, with abortions and obsessions—she tried to recover in art. If, as one poem has it, art is a cracked looking glass, it shows us the "Grand ceremonials of a play / By which we tried to live a passion out / By every nuance in a little room." That little room is, finally, the stanza of a poem. And that mirror—image of the widened eye opposite and of the cloud-crossed moon outside—is, like the poem, a witchery held up to see one's secret life in, and "though the smoke is gone there is some fire / In saying so."

"The Grand Canyon" has been singled out by some critics as Garrigue's finest poem. Certainly it is her most virtuosic. There are just four sentences, but one of them swirls through 109 lines. That sentence begins with the phrase "I am lonely" and then fills up with an astonishing plenitude of descriptive and speculative detail. *Facts, things*—cliffs and roots and wedges of shadow—inhibit her confrontation with the Sublime, which is the poem's true subject. Garrigue was teaching on the West Coast in 1971 and fell seriously ill. She was diagnosed with Hodgkin's disease and decided to return to the East for treatment. She had just a year left to live (she died on December 27, 1972), and it was on that slow, anxious cross-country trip that she stopped to visit the Grand Canyon. With those facts in mind, as they are not in the poem, it is hard not to scrutinize the scene differently. In the very first stanza, for instance, there is an ordinary observation that turns menacing: "the raven that flies, scouring above it, / of the hooked face and the almost flat sleek wings." Then notice how the foreboding seeps into the next lines:

> I am lonely,
> knocked out, stunned-sleepy,
> knocked out by the terraced massed faces
> of the brute Sublime,
> color inflamed,
> when I came to the edge and looked over:
> violaceous, vermillion
> great frontal reefs, buttes,
>
> cliffs of rufous and ocher angles,
> promontories, projections, jutments, outjuttings

and gnarled mirlitons, so it seemed,
twisting up out of depth beyond depth
gnarled like the juniper tree
rachitic with wind I hung on to
as the raven's wing, glassy in the light of its black,
slid over me . . .

"This maw, gash / deepest in the world," then, is death itself—Emptiness and Nothing, at once infernal and alluring. Perhaps to defend herself against the merely personal in this poem, Garrigue structured the episode in wholly lyric terms. This was not a woman confronting her own mortality, though that is a powerful and troubling undercurrent; instead, she devised an altogether grander, nearly mythological encounter. It is a poem about what she called "threshholds." Faced with a "stillness / stinging, overpowering the ear, / pure condition of the original echoing soundlessness," she stepped into words, stepped up to the poet's task: naming, describing, praising in an ecstatic burst of language.

Though it may be her best poem, "The Grand Canyon" is not finally a characteristic one, just as the lyric is not in the end her truest voice. "Studies for an Actress," a sort of refracted self-portrait, veers through thoughts, through baffling powers she would appease and could not, through unsatisfied memories and emblematic longings. The pageant of dreamwork, the puzzle of the will as it rushes at love, those mysterious ways by which the self is assembled and sustained— Garrigue threaded her way through these mazes with a series of questions, testing each step and in the end surrendering to the very process itself:

She prays if nothing else to be
In some dissolving medium of light,
A pond that's set to catch the arrowy beams,
Reflective and obedient as that.
She prays then to change
If it's in changing that things find repose.

She prays to praise. She prays to be
Condensed now to one desire
As if it were very life performing her.

"The dialogue of self with soul, the quarrel of self with world"
is how Garrigue once described her work, and she wanted a language
"which takes its rhythms from heartbeat and blood." Only to be in-
trigued by the sumptuary textures of her verse is to risk missing the
sharply dramatic nature of her poems. It was not Marianne Moore to
whom Garrigue looked as a model (though she wrote a critical study
of Moore), but Emily Dickinson; she admired Moore but identified
with Dickinson. In an essay about Dickinson that clearly projects the
impulses of her own imagination, Garrigue linked her with Donne
and the other metaphysicals who "had fed on awe":

> The unattainable was her passion and her woe, her ecstatic bereave-
> ment, that loss she gets strange gain from. That restless mind, driven to
> an extremity and, visited by velocities of intuition, a kind of victim of
> its own phosphorescent gleanings from the seas of the dimensions she
> perished but survived in. Is she not odd, oblique, quivering, overstrung,
> "blue-peninsulaed"? . . . No substances were common for her. She saw
> them all as rare. Her effort was to achieve the language that would
> allow their rareness to be known. . . . Dramatic rather than lyrical, she
> is direct, vigorous, and so original that she suffered for it throughout
> her lifetime.

Garrigue heard Dickinson's language as dissonant, compressed, an-
gular, introspective, yet suited for conflict and above all flamboyantly
emotional.

In Garrigue's view, love, death, and poetry were for Dickin-
son parts of a trinity that meet at the "junction of Eternity." Yet
Garrigue's own last collection, though it triangulates these abiding
themes, is also her most engaged and timely work. *Studies for an Ac-
tress,* published posthumously in 1973, marks the third stage, or full
maturity, of her art. There are elegies and love letters, but also politi-
cal meditations. It is true that her early books included poems like

"That Fascist Bird" and "V-J Day," but politics are their occasion, not their subject. Her late poems, on the other hand, although they cast a cold eye on "our swollen pigsfoot of a state," are never merely polemical. As Adrienne Rich once observed about them, Garrigue "evokes a sense of contemporary helplessness, not merely before shattering public events, but individual reticence and disrelation." The most important relationship in Garrigue's life was her long and troubled liaison with the radical novelist Josephine Herbst, who died in 1969. It may have been Herbst who awakened Garrigue's political conscience. "You would have it that we may break out of ourselves," Garrigue wrote in her elegy for Herbst, "the solitude breaking down also." But the times themselves—the late 1960s—were volatile, and Garrigue was a thinking woman. History had raided her dreameries. In the face of "friends retreating into wordlessness . . . Like love going back on what it'd said and sworn," she felt impelled to defend clarity against deceit, to confront "the crooked coldness, emptiness / That slacks the purpose in a waste of war," to bear witness to "the pain of others beginning to show through." Her outraged moral conscience— as she dramatized it in "Resistance Meeting: Boston Common"— was finally an extension of her threatened sense of self, her vulnerable sense of romantic poethood:

> An order that has always been known,
> known, forgotten, denied
> under the pressure not to distinguish what is true from what is
>   necessary,
> flying the flag of expediency,
> which is the mere power of the mind
> or the idea, the pure idea of man
> witness on his own terms to what he knows,
> making and re-making what he is.

For all its poise and precision, its new commitments and curiosities, *Studies for an Actress* remains a charged example of what Jane Mayhall once rightly called Garrigue's "reckless grandeur." The book's serenity is counterbalanced by a "myth-making mist and resurrecting light." Hoping to make the glitter break into song in her late poem "Moondial," Garrigue reminds us that "we are animals of the moon." By its light we are permitted flashing glimpses of both the chaos and the order at the heart of things. Here are trees, dressed in moonlight:

> Perfect they stood and were the more perfected
> We thanked the light for falling as it did
> To show their every tangle in the whole
> Of wildest, most cross-flowing intricacy.
> Such wildness asked for ceremony.

A wildness that evokes ceremony goes to the heart of Jean Garrigue's imagination. "I like comets, lightning, fireworks," she once confessed—and might as well have been describing her preference for Wyatt, Donne, Marvell, Hopkins, Yeats, Hart Crane, and Dylan Thomas. It was by flashes of lightning that she wrote, the true Romantic poet of her generation. "My salvation," she confided to her notebook, "is in moments; by actions of perception and redemption." Her notebooks are filled with such self-revealing sketches: "Still kept from the feast I tremble before the crumb that falls and my hunger makes that a feast." *The moment, the flash, the crumb—* these are what she took up into her great hunger. "Where to begin the poem?" she asked. "As close as you can to the nerve." *Hunger, nerve, grandeur*—these are what she gave back. At the end of her life, in her great poem of departure, "Grief Was to Go Out, Away," she is alone on a beach, and like Whitman or Elizabeth Bishop in similar poems, she broods over what she must abandon:

> Grief was just in the having
> Of so much heart pulse gone out and away
> Into absence and the spent shadow
> Of what ran from our fingers as ripples
> Of shadow over the sand and what eluded
> In a bending of mirrors the tipped tints and reflections

And was just so much running down the packed sands'
Mile-wide blondness of bird-tracked floor.

    The enormity of the ambition, the splendor of the achievement—both make more poignant still one simple entry in her notebook, where the poet looked back on her own career: "I lived for certain grandeurs that fade fast—me, JG."

J. D. McClatchy

FROM

*Thirty-Six Poems and
a Few Songs*

(1944)

From Venice Was That Afternoon

From Venice was that afternoon
Though it was our land's canal we viewed.
There willows clove the bluish heat
By dropping leaf or two, gold green
And every tuft of hill beyond
Stood bright, distinct, as if preserved
By glass that sealed out light but not
Its gold or influence.
And floated on the speckled stream
A child of brilliant innocence
Where on the docks of green we stood
Naming it Love for its perfection.
This seemed to be . . .
But the current carried the leaves swiftly,
So flowed that child away from us,
So stared we sternly at the water's empty face.
Ah, in the greenhouse of that hour
Waited in the tare and sorrel
The mouth of fleshliness that stopped:
The leaves that dappled on that breast
The five-sensed image of our pleasance
Have now destroyed its lineaments.
For the waters of that afternoon
Flowed through Negation's glassy land
Where, in this civil, gate-closed hour
The verges of those waters now
Drown that joy that was our power.
What tyranny imposed this pride
That caused love's gift to be denied
And our destroying features to
Cast perpetually on its brow
The glass accepting no leaves now?
In rages of the intellect
We gave to heaven abstinence
Who said our love must issue from

No cisterns of the ruddy sun
But like the artifice of fountains
Leap from cold, infertile sources.
And our destroying features thus
Cast from that land its beingness
And strewed upon the green-fleshed hills
Sands of our darkening great ills.

The Stranger

Now upon this piteous year
I sit in Denmark beside the quai
And nothing that the fishers say
Or the children carrying boats
Can recall me from that place
Where sense and wish departed me
Whose very shores take on
The whiteness of anon.
For I beheld a stranger there
Who moved ahead of me
So tensile and so dancer made
That like a thief I followed her
Though my heart was so alive
I thought it equal to that beauty.
But when at last a turning came
Like the branching of a river
And I saw if she walked on
She would be gone forever,
Fear, then, so wounded me
As fell upon my ear
The voice a blind man dreams
And broke on me the smile
I dreamed as deaf men hear,
I stood there like a spy,
My tongue and eyelids taken
In such necessity.
Now upon this piteous year
The rains of Autumn fall.
Where may she be?
I suffered her to disappear
Who hunger in the prison of my fear.
That lean and brown, that stride,
That cold and melting pride,
For whom the river like a clear

Melodic line and the distant carrousel
Where lovers on their beasts of play
Rose and fell,
That wayfare where the swan adorned
With every wave and eddy
The honor of his sexual beauty,
Create her out of sorrow
That, never perishing,
Is a stately thing.

The Brook

The brook contains its landing under water.
There each leaf above is thus
Engrossed by shadows under
Nor there the stone can sunder
Filaments that make the structure.
There hang harebell's noose
Blue-peaked, and strung moss.
All is underneath the brook
Face, a building made by shadow,
No architecture of the seen
Shimmered as on earth we know.
There shades are most substantial,
Closing out the fish whose plumes
Would make beautiful,
And the sandy minnow.
But as the ambitious fly must go
Into the spider's castle
To be preservèd there
Until the castle's center
Moves upon the venturer,
So I dreamed in my buried wish
My naked senses went
That underwater's still grandeur.
I dreamed in that most glassy web
I touched with woven breast
Those galleries of glass,
Feeding invisibly on life
As insects use the membrane of the water.

The Clovers

For the heart, willing and not willing,
Is glassed under as clover in a stand of storm water.
In the downy sink of the ground
Rain is an inch deep over the heads of those four leaves
And the sides turn silver in the embossed
Pond-meadow. Think of a whole army of clover
Hidden under, lace all, green as an apple.

For the heart, willing and not willing,
Stands in a rain-settle too, transparent
To all in a vale, where the firm skin of wish
Dapples and lines it
And its veins are exposed, pale
To the tremble of world's rage, ail,
But not sky is reflected nor sun from the gray pall of heaven,
Not seed whistling by nor bird dipping.

Transparency has its savior, visible and invisible!
For as the clover stem suggests no relation
To its top parent, and under that water
Leaves stay in a stitching, sewn like a cobbled silk,
So the heart, as obscurely rooted
Is as rooted, though with a pretty way
It lies in the film of flesh, a marrow of constancy.

But nor sun reaches to nor strengthens by air
That fond delicacy
And the dwarf hidden roots, apparent to none,
Obstruct the dark muscle, a clarity upside
But a dark land thereunder,
Willing, unwilling, ignorant and imitator,
In the source of that woodland, the improvident flood.

The Circle

The wood, swollen with mushrooms,
Those rotting like excrement,
Those blooming in monkey scarlet,
Branch-brown and butter yellow,
The wood, swollen with voices,
Those high-blood, tortured sexual cries,
The penitential voice singing,
The wood, branch-brown, branched with weeping:

Who am I, am I,
Where the mirror has splashed its bloodless blood,
Who am I in the bloodless wood?
I said: eternity is this:
The formless past within the glass,
The flesh deprived of its true lust,
The inward virtue of the flesh
Corroded by the formless past,
I said: damnation is this eternity,
The mind divorced at last from act,
Distracted senses caged now judged,
Those thumping ranters damned who drag
The battered actor through such mire,
The act full-judged but not altered
(The crooked blood cannot run straight)
Perversity steals the old color
And red runs white in secret ill.

I said: eternity is this travel
Around and round the center of the wood,
Beset by cries, the sullied pool,
The light of mushrooms, moths running
As large as mice on the forest floor,
The flesh, that battered animal,

Asserting its ample sty has dignity.
I said: eternity devours the mind,
Devours and cannot change by its devouring,
The outward terror remains the same,
And the wood, swollen with mushrooms, the dark wood.

Waking, I Always Waked You Awake

Waking, I always waked you awake
As always I fell from the ledge of your arms
Into the soft sand and silt of sleep
Permitted by you awake, with your arms firm.

Waking, always I waked immediately
To the face you were when I was off sleeping,
Ribboned with sea weed or running with deer
In a valentine country of swans in the door.

Waking, always waked to the tasting of dew
As if my sleep issued tears for its loving
Waking, always waked, swimming from foam
Breathing from mountains clad in a cloud.

As waking, always waked in the health of your eyes,
Curled your leaf hair, uncovered your hands,
Good morning like birds in an innocence
Wild as the Indies we ever first found.

The Mouse

When the mouse died at night
He was all overgrown with delight,
His whiskers thick as a wood
From exploring the Polar cupboard
And his eyes still agape
From risky accomplishment.
No honor or drum was his bait.
The more glorious, he
Who with no shame for time
Then boldly died,
Three weeks a rich spell
Of sound and pure smell
And all his long leisure
For meat of short measure
(An ant could carry it.)
Praise him who sweetens
On a small hate.

Forest

There is the star bloom of the moss
And the hairy chunks of light between the conifers;
There are alleys of light where the green leads to a funeral
Down the false floor of needles.
There are rocks and boulders that jut, saw-toothed and urine-yellow.
Other stones in a field look in the distance like sheep grazing,
Grey trunk and trunklike legs and lowered head.
There are short-stemmed forests so close to the ground
You would pity a dog lost there in the spore-budding
Blackness where the sun has never struck down.
There are dying ferns that glow like a gold mine
And weeds and sumac extend the Sodom of color.
Among the divisions of stone and the fissures of branch
Lurk the abashed resentments of the ego.
Do not say this is pleasurable!
Bats, skittering on wires over the lake,
And the bug on the water, bristling in light as he measures forward
    his leaps,
The hills holding back the sun by their notched edges
(What volcanoes lie on the other side
Of heat, light, burning up even the angels)
And the mirror of forests and hills drawing nearer
Till the lake is all forests and hills made double,
Do not say this is kindly, convenient,
Warms the hands, crosses the senses with promise,
Harries our fear.
Uneasy, we bellow back at the tree frogs
And, night approaching like the entrance of a tunnel,
We would turn back and cannot, we
Surprise our natures; the woods lock us up
In the secret crimes of our intent.

With Glaze of Tears

With glaze of tears or of
Madness, our eyelids winged
The land: tall clouds reflected
Upon us, grass blowing in
Glint of cloud, rock, scene of
Our meetings, pathways around
The fen.
Looking into this lucid
Scene flowing beneath us, sight
Dimmed; as if the synapses
Splintered, sight darkened and failed.
For our landscape of love was
Neither each other's features
Since we were each other, but
Rich and violent country.
It was our love's and our
Soul's figuration. Now,
To stand in this separation
From cloud and flower of our kin,
Now in our seeking to close out
All spaces our eyes had run,
To know this land was symbol,
Ethereal, which had fed our veins,
Was ailing of being, was staring
To breathe flower's air or
Flower of us? Confusion trebled.
Leaping and leaping our hearts,
Sight staggered; if landscape was
Different than we, so were we,
So were we, falling, ourselves from
Ourselves cut off, emblem of love
Torn in two.

FROM

The Ego and the Centaur

(1947)

Primer of Plato

All endeavor to be beautiful:
The loved and the loveless as well:
All women rob from duty's time
To pitch adornment to its prime.
The lion in his golden coat
Begets his joy by that; his mate
Beneath that fiery mane repeats
The fury of each sudden sense.
The swan reflecting on the stream
The opposite feathers of the swan-
Webbed dream is like the fox at night
Who glows as in original delight.
Not least, the sun in tedious round
Bestows on rock and land
Principles that all creation
Imitates in adoration.

I never knew this till I
Chanced to see how your bright cheek
Brightened from the gaze of one
Whose spirit swam a Hellespont.
I saw then that beauty was
Both for lover and beloved a feast,
The lover mirroring by his joy
That flush beauty brings, in
His eye her actual face globed small,
And beauty flattered by that glass
Pitched to its highest comeliness,
Doubled and increased until
All would seem
Derived back into first essence.
Both animals and men dwell
In such a mirror of the real

Until in sudden ecstasy
They break the boundaries of that glass
To be the image each first was.

Iowa City Zoo

That ring-necked pheasant, feather-worn,
Drinks water grey-scummed, his snake eye
Sullen in no gratitude, leaves thick on wire
Of chicken cage; the sun falls in
Through escaped feathers and the taint of leaves.
It's arbitrary, that roof the Autumn's blown.

Delicately the rabbit drinking catches
His chin hairs there; they're limp from weight.
A black wife hunches in the farther dark.
The turkey hens are crying frugally,
Their heads in a maze of discontent.
Shoo their turkey-cocks toward them!

Look: their dirty runways, races, water,
Their leaky houses, battered turnips, grain
Rotting (mauve doves peck at the soiling floor,
Their eyes diamonded by curious zest—the blood
That shines there through the eye?). What dignity
Affronts offal! Security that cannot be disarmed!

But wall-eyed deer, the lilacs fed you well.
Since you are blind, your eyes are all of us.
When will we trip and fall upon their look,
That bugled eye, that marble-sick uniqueness?
The rabbit's shamed who drinks dewfall
And you in your detention here
Have dulled our natures with your spartan glitter,
As misery embarrasses the poor.

Song

O beautiful, my relic bone,
Whitening like the foreign moon,
Whose luster consummates my tomb.

O beautiful, my flesh rose-grown,
Rose-rose white from that small bone
Whose vapor is the breath I own

And tendrils of my blood curl in.
Rose-rose white, the flesh I am
But murderer eye and murdered!

For all the flesh becomes an eye:
I am no flesh while yet eye's eaten
The rose-rose flesh bare to the bone,

Bare to the bone! But that flesh still
By heat of dews renews again.

O bless, occurrence of the moon
When actual flesh of both is gone,
My flesh the air the eye takes in,

That flesh on bone the air the eye takes in,
Death-wedding the moon shines in.

Homage to Ghosts

Always within me lies
That former form of experience
If suddenly I bare my eyes.
Always dismembering me, although
It is so altered and so changed
I know it and know it not.
O, I ponder that time set
Some things beneath its yoke
And set not it
And yet my passion and my want
Built a lasting place wherein
Obediently it lies
And still evades all consequence
Of an ordinary demise.

But I see that even mind
Alters substance between time.
In those years it has lain there
I grew different, and my change,
All unknowing, made it strange.
The image that it lay in me
Was subject as I was to all
Shocks that made my soul grow ill,
Took account of every sorrow,
And of my body did so borrow
Till I think that what was it
Is now, surely, only me.

Still, it has such separate power
It forbids all I would touch
And takes away the life from what
Is living, though it is not.
Perhaps it is my tomb as well,
For both of us without conjunction

Lie prison stones on recollection.
But thought, despite such memory,
Yet tears the soul from the body.
I love and do not love
And indifference and fidelity
Between their greeds fast with me,
My bones plucked dry to satisfy
That double eternity.

The Mask and Knife

And I would have you clad like dominoes
In every stripe and lozenge you would dare,
A gauged discord, irregular and clair,
Or corsleted in ribands like a beau.

Be armed by shells, those profits of the Sound,
As slippered like a prince in modesty
You softly fly the docks as coarse sail cloth
Swelled by the wind and sailing bluely north.

O jacketed like jockeys in a silk!
I'd have you rayed and tangled in douce ropes
Where hawsers found their ships at captive ports.
Odor of fur, a belle cool din!

Till when the shock of some dark pose
Makes leapt commotion like a white furore
Of one wave, only one wave seen
Raging on the night-paned seas

Or as the Spring unwinds the flood
Or as a perfume galls the scrupled blood
And you have yoked me till I cannot break
Though broken I as uncouth horsemen might

Bully a spirit to its brink.
And your very name—its lips make weights in me.

Only the Irresistible Abides

At the crossing, wind-stricken in blow, I saw
Him of dead cares in penal fire.
The wind foully fell; the dung of the bird dropped.

Rough was the blast; rough clove bones to the beat
Flesh in such charge, shift.
Leaves drove backwards and forwards,
The horse reared; in the near distance sheep nudged,
Seeking determination of their warmth.

Crying aloud, my voice was snatched
Only to be tossed high like a leaf, empty
The word returned to my struck mouth.
Clearly going into my heart, had rolled back
His brow from its torment, his eyes from their penance.
What matter, cry of the wind hissing,
Sucking his face?
To my heart I trembled as radically changed the nature of him,
Spoliation, the bitter air of corruption.
Foresaw strength devoured by the weakness it came forth from,
The eye, flag of the war,
Dark light of the head, dark, hovered blood,
Cut tear, maniacal pity,
The smile bled by its subtleties there,
Killed pang, satirical mercy,
Sleep dead; the mouth closed like a grave upon
Traitorous censors, sweet frauds, hypocrites of the heart.

We passed; breath torn, bleeding,
I was at raw rock, dark the pit, roaring.
Foresaw his daemons with whom he contended.
Foresaw his battle running against him,
For the delicate conscience alone has embraced defeat,
Saw in spite of the issue always in question,
His lion-like labor.

Love, like those shadowy starlings wailing,
Plunged against buildings, their blind bodies falling,
Love, born to my breast, rose, more rugged
Than gust, blast, instructing his tyrants,
Of his abyss defiant,
Courier caught sweet blood of his tears, sweet anguish wrung,
As his name I came to through valleys of evil, of honor
Resisting no evil nor knowledge that the soul endeavor
World in him.

Enemy of Those Who Are Enemies of Sleep

O moon my mask,
Clear in the nightwoods now you lie,
Tilted upon your halved and garroted face.

O moon my mask,
Dealer of actions lewd and forced,
Upon the unlettered waste,

O moon, sweet task, white face,
O white, O sweet, my oval glance,
I turn, I turn, from your empowering glass.

O now . . . for whose engrossing force . . .
Although by pitchpine you are borne
Or tusked by mountains you are flung,

Your leafage, play, your stamps of intricacy,
O moon, intemperate tenement, convict
Like a clown's great gloves, the trademark

For, or hairy maps and biscuits of
Day's convert dragging us through pits.
O moon, sweet angelology of fall,

Your parts and terminals of light,
Before you're out, must win, despite . . .
For in our sleep you breed our dreams for us

Half children of your sensual tyranny,
By whose Urania gods and cats
In equal heat, conciliate your snows

And we, by your sphered music, top
White forms, fair senses, eastern genii that
Launch summers just as soundlessly

As all the engines of eternity.
O nuptial drug and condiment of rite,
O tempter to an inwardness of sight,

Dwarfs, indigo, within whose opera,
O bridal jest, you circummortal us,
Nuptial of vacancy who wizards us.

And all the fur of suns is not worth you
Burning in empty hamlets our abstracts
Whose shadows close behind us like a door.

Poem

I saw the mountains in a rose-fire light
Upon my ill-housed street, whose old-law flats
Were stained a blood light, rose-christ light.
Those mountains of the sun I saw,

All peaked and small, like waves that stabilize
Their pearl, or crystallize into a snow
Their light, all cast aboundingly from out
The fiery brim, the golden den of night.

As if a skiey flame could crucify
Our lives, the prisons of conceptual plight,
I saw, I wept, for we were all burning,
Our faces all, in crucibles of light.

Immutable vision of the beautiful
That changes once and once again with light!
A cloud cast on the sun its ire,
That flaming and descending sun did then depart
And it was gray, the first of night.

I saw how easily we start—
Our hearts in us that so desire the fire
I saw and wept and we were all.
I saw and wept, my cheek did burn

Vision and illusion, Oh return!
That I with joy and fire and light
In fire and light and delicate joy my life
May live in crucibles like that, and burn.

False Country of the Zoo

We are large with pity, slow and awkward
In the false country of the zoo.
For the beasts our hearts turn over and sigh,
With the gazelle we long to look eye to eye,
Laughter at the stumbling, southern giraffes
Urges our anger, righteous despair.
As the hartebeest plunges, giddy, eccentric,
From out of the courtyard into his stall,
We long to seize his forehead's steep horns
Which are like the staves of a lyre.
Fleeter than greyhounds the hartebeest
Long-muzzled, small-footed, and shy.
Another runner, the emu, is even better
At kicking. Oh, the coarse chicken feet
Of this bird reputed a fossil!
His body, deep as a table,
Droops gracelessly downwise,
His small head shakes like an old woman's eye.
The emu, the ostrich, the cassowary
Continue to go on living their lives
In conditions unnatural to them
And in relations most strange
Remain the same.
As for the secretary bird,
Snake-killer, he suggests
A mischievous bird-maker.
Like a long-legged boy in short pants
He runs teetering, legs far apart,
On his toes, part gasping girl.
What thought him up, this creature
Eminently equipped by his nervous habits
To kill venomous snakes with his strong
Horny feet, first jumping on them
And then leaping away?
At the reptile and monkey houses

Crowds gather to enjoy the ugly
But mock the kangaroo who walks like a cripple.

In the false country of the zoo,
Where Africa is well represented
By Australia,
The emu, the ostrich and cassowary
Survive like kings, poor antiquated strays,
Deceased in all but vestiges,
Who did not have to change, preserved
In their peculiarities by rifts,
From emigration barred.
Now melancholy, like old continents
Unmodified and discontinued, they
Remain by some discreet permission
Like older souls too painfully handicapped.
Running birds who cannot fly,
Whose virtue is their liability,
Whose stubborn very resistance is their sorrow.
See, as they run, how we laugh
At the primitive, relic procedure.

In the false country of the zoo
Grief is well represented there
By those continents of the odd
And outmoded, Africa and Australia.
Sensation is foremost at a zoo—
The sensation of gaping at the particular:
The striped and camouflaged,
The bear, wallowing in his anger,
The humid tiger wading in a pool.
As for those imports
From Java and India,
The pale, virginal peafowl,
The stork, cracking his bill against a wall,

The peacock, plumes up, though he walks as if weighted
—All that unconscionable tapestry—
Till a wind blows the source of his pride
And it becomes his embarrassment,
The eye, plunged in sensation, closes.
Thought seizes the image. This shrieking
Jungle of spot, stripe, orange
Blurs. The oil from the deer's eye
That streaks like a tear his cheek
Seems like a tear, is, is,
As our love and our pity are, are.

The Monument
Rose

(1953)

The Strike of the Night

Fate, heat, the strike of the night,
It is all seen inward in time.
We love what we love for ill or good
It is the fascination of what is done
And we are blood, blood
Moves in our mind. Is it blind, blind?
Is as well, wine. Is it doom? As much
Song. And the night plucks open our veins,
Strong, strong.

In the garden the roses scattered
When under the wickets I came
To their blooming there on the mound.
Such early largesse of red
Succeeding the flags overthrown!
Bees rolling in golden cups
And the Persian wine of those pinks
Crossing the sense with their powders, oils
To be pressed in the prime
Of the year's still white and green
Till I saw a wreath cast down.
There, what a spectre tomb!
In the shape of the dwindled moon.

For all the unborn, it sang, a song.
For those who are about to die, another
One. A song or son, laughed the worm.

There was into the nights this blood
Slaughtered by seasons, the pent-up fume
Dislodging its petals one by one
In the liquefaction of June.

But I was in the pale of the wood

Before I saw what I understood
And after, at the door of the west,
Before there struck and clanged my breast.

Gravepiece

It is there where the worm has egress
That I prod these bones in their lair
And would push them out of their proper place
To find the vivid core

The heart I pried from the worm's small jaws
When I spied the nail
And its intricate system of holding down the dead
Who weary of the grave's moist hell

Now other than the worm may pulp and tear
For I threw it out of its grinning clothes
It is my heart that runs among these bones
And the virid excess of the enormous hair

In the dead of night the dogs that had the heart
To seize the heart I threw (and rived the air)
Will come with the mangled thing afire on their tongues
And find me out where I stacked the bones

And made a crosstree from the thigh's long ones
Such fire will burst my swound in a shift of bones
Crippled with one for a crutch I will come forth
In the dead of night the dogs will find us both

We will hang on the cross and chatter of love in the winds.

The Maimed Grasshopper Speaks Up

I have three simple eyes
Perceiving love, death, and hate
Up close, as insects do,
Who thrive by the particular view.

The biggest eyes, with armor on,
That gave me fore and backward sight
Into the ditches of rash thought
Serve me not, the armor's broke.

Thus I may not leap which way
Into the truths of enemy
Or love's fool's ruddy cave
Or the inscrutable world's vault

Lest the rude, simple feelers break.
Thought asks for eyes that see all round
And make its parts to jump the moon,
Monument leapers, leopards of intellect.

Universalists of sight,
I to that moon am like the blind
Who may but feel, not see its light.
And thus in destitution sit.

World without end, commend me to your might
That I my simple eyes may set
On it, or death, or hate, and get some light.

Invocation to Old Windylocks

That blue, that dark, dark, green-dark blue,
That knolled dome and cone, magnetic sphere
Whose rough-edged line's an adamant composed
By this sheer falling of the world's line here
Of continents, the clouds, now mapped and cloven,
Breast, cleft, and magnanimities
Whose boughs are earth, whose earth is air,
Air, light, that blue, that dark, dark, green-dark blue
And weight, whose dark sides trammel me

That blue, that dark, dark, green-dark blue
By this mid-sunlight pierced whose shafts and rifts
From delicate armories thinned do bend
Across the dredged green crest:
Wave steadfast, graven in the unstained clear
Refractive of the earth's rapt atmosphere—
Paladin rim-foiled, centurion
Of the untrodden distance, suspiration of stars,
Whose gaze now holds us, fixed and pierced,
To this obstacle's strict post
The energy of our unearthly hopes!—
That is dark-blue, that is dark-green blue,
Flesh of timber wrung through
As lilac enflasked in its smoky color
Gives up on the white alphabet of the river—

That is dark-blue, that is dark-green blue
Upon whose edge the sunlight falls and swifts
Exhumed, say, from a dark crop of violets,
Intricate outlaying embased
Upon the blue and white enfolded
Of the very centuries impounded
That at the tag-ends of such space—

Thy steeps and falls, thy rigor

Curled, pressing out of the world,
Where not even the bee stings
Though the wind wallows in troughs of cloud
Winking like leaves whose tops are similar nests—

Configuration of weight, heat, energy
Anchoring the sky in exhalations almighty
Thy stroked slopes and downs,
Thy amorous sides enshaped by air,
In the perspectives of hailed eternity!

By the sworn vapors where we turn
Turned, falling, to fall upon
When by optic we tremble at the cliff,
Pock-marks of the delirious distance
As if from a cloud! we rode, the eye
Astride its surface on a reined-out wind—

If to look were to touch, move, be.
Perspective in thy light as to
In the revolutions of ecstasy
Precipitate that green, that dark elixir

And in the sharp wood and shadow
Inverted upon thy pastures
To go all up and down, to embrace thee,
Traversed, translucent slopes, or bird-gods we
To thy light's four round declivities—

Night birth of cloud, to be
In the delirium of mists or thy clear sea—
Diamond cast forth from the earth's rage,
Rarefied arrogance beside whom
The clear star rests and reigns,

Deep in the midsummer casque of flesh
Exalted, secret, calm, and vast, to stay—
Into which the night clambers and the day—
Thicket entangled, up which in ropy ascent
Vapors in the clear fervors of morning rest
Like a mid-Norway

And we held to thee, infatuate on thy flank
Great prow, aerial bulk,
Florilegium, stepping forth into fresh-running light,
Arcana coelestia.

Address to the Migrations

A pounding on wood. The woodpecker.
The turfed castle of ants. The weeds very still.
It is autumn and I lie on the ground
In the thin pelt of the sun.
The sky is low and sealed around
With doors and walls of clouds rippled like shells.
Autumnal whiteness thins and rarefies,
I lie in the strawy wood and close my eyes.
All would be silent but that pods
Break and seeds let go.
A burring of wings in papery weeds.
I would sleep in the sling of autumn till white snow
Sifted and fulfilled its dying saws
Of insects pitching and leaping at wild doors.
And sumptuary laws. Suspension of stillness
While there draws, flying and lighting,
Streamers of seeds.
A chill befalls me when they fall.
By death? By death? In the henna fields?
Or sleepy death preparing his long mills?
Suddenly all over the fields a barking of crows.
While far above, it seems, a strangeness sails
Or delicate strangeness calls. It is not to be heard.
These are imagined cries.
And I awake to go and turn and rise.
There is a black thread in the skies
Notched like an arrow and it streams from clouds.
Peaks let it go.
Now wind to wind the sky is filled with some
Tremor and echo, intervals
Staying and falling you cannot hear—
Bugled communion! panging up the air
Or already flight is so fast flight pangs the ear.
The line comes near, thin as a hair
And some fly there back of its prow

And some fly riffling the shaft's seamed edge that reams the air
Till the sky seems cut and clouds part there
Or is it air raveling these ranks? It pulls faster
Till on the wheel of some vast round veers left.
The stook of the sun stands here and further walls.
One instant more and it has plunged past, gone—
Door beyond door, leaving the whole sky-rift,
Atlantic vistas, depthless drifts beyond drifts.
Now lumber up and would flop after, crows
Like spies the country wished of rearguard thought,
Loosed feathers from the shaft that drove.
My turfed castle of ants is busy . . .

Line, sign, glyph out of time,
Ancestries of language riding, this writing,
Once on the pearly beachhead of the day
We saw you there.
Animal ravings towered the air. Hounds
And the tame birds bayed and clapped their claws
And I, I hailed and cried
Some divination yielding up its laws
Nor know I line of music or of words
Sent from the shaft more perfectly across
This body of the world than that brief race
Seen for an instant there in the immense.

For Anybody's Martyr's Song

What's love that's always strong?
Beasts from the Antipodes spring down!
And hoydens leap like lions over beaches!
Love is the friend whose faithfulness is wit,
Is best your mimic when you tongue-tied vow,
Aloof when you win and surly when you stammer,
Cries I do not understand you, and
Corrects your right answer.

Indulges with contempt your sweet tooth at the fair,
Gives you fearful rides on the roller coaster,
Greets you like a sovereign when you've come
An hour, but puts the green toad in your bed
Just as soon thereafter.
Your sober love turns tomcat in the bar.

Children hate school, soldiers discipline
Love hates love but what's the good of that?
Oh the sweet cry, the dark eye!
Love stamps its foot but cannot slip the knot.

Nor can remove the leopard's spot
Nor ever dye the wolf white,
Love loves what love is
Nor can it change that.

There Is a Dark River

There is a dark river flows under a bridge
Making an elbowed turn where the swallows skim
Indescribably dark in rain.
You think of the Floss, drifting down
To the boyhood of the implacable maelstrom
And a boathouse rotting in shadow.
The grapes of Concord are thick with hawthorn
And the old manse is ripe with the eaved rain.

There is a dark river under a bridge
Where beyond, grasses stand up
Most English lone at the wide bend.
Those oblivion-haunted ones who wrote
Memorable words on the window pane.
What but the diamond's firmness gives them name?
And yet because they did it
The field is thick with spirit.

Across from this rich running a crop
Under the pines of black-toothed stones.
Happy the lilacs; happy each stem
By the troughs of the green sunk down.
Something other than animal dread
Made us pray when we stood by them
That this same love with the full of thought
Go down and touch at the base of the root
The unutterable, which is unmortal.

There is a dark river flows under a bridge
Where the reeds stand in the come and go
Of a boathouse black in the shadow.
Here swallows fly over its swirl.
A wild gyre of midges below.
There by the tremble of water

Spectres whom we might know
Stand chanting of what we no longer
May read the text for, in the shadow.

And yet the color of their tears is over the water
And the air is plunged into echo
Of their long eyes in the mirror.
Do we not see this, do we not know—
There in the gliding below
Is not the sight slanted with thought
Of this same willow from which they drank.

Rich-running water, indescribably much
Emblackened by wild-running years
As at nightfall when clamor thickens
All the night over with sleeping things,
Invisible footfalls and murmurings—

Here where the swallows drink from the bend
Shadows our shadows stir
In the trepidation of light
That the down-reaching boughs collect
Ah! To feel is to understand
Here in the to and fro
Of what looks forth and what glides over
How all might recur again,
So rich the tremble there seems to wed
Kingdoms of flesh and shade.

A Water Walk by
Villa d'Este

(1959)

One for the Roses

My dancing roses, dancing in November,
Your red more deepened for the sun has waned,
The frost is black on the grass, green-gray the ice,
And still within this court you dance.

And yet your petals toughened by the cold,
Bowed in the grass like small-clothes dropped,
The bud most champfered where the cheek was rich
As mildest infants in their sleep of lace,

My dancing roses, dancing in November,
Parterre, parlance, my rose plantation,
When winds that start the hectic sting and chill,
Pierce me with thorns still pliant and still green

Though fallen is the nest and honeycomb,
That butterfly, it barely fans the light,
And numb the wasp, the bee drowsy
Though still serene, half-rapt

Because he's near his parcels yet
Of providences left,
If I be not the witness of your reign,
Your scarlet like a vintage the decree

Your fallen petals now its seal
To undertake as faithfuls do, the fire
Of how you flourish on the year's deathbed.
So, temperate queens, upon that sighing-out

There on the short cold grass when wind has come
Up to your green-hinged knees and snow has blown
Those lovely crowns you wore the half-year long,
To spurn with your valor, and by red singe white.

Not that I seek the moral, rose,
Nor preach to you from rostrums, dear,
Whose dial marks the umbering of the year,
But that the way you stain and dye the air

Banked with the hedgerow of the plum and gold
Is peerless, and more mad than ruin.
To walk among your tiers where the dew is cold,
Your damson signet and your green my rule,

As, on that morning when the wind comes
Blowing a cloud of snow up to your leaves
And crowns on whom the wind expounds, to say:
I have beheld you in your dominion, rose,

And you are light and day.

A Mourning

(for Dylan Thomas)

The day was unbearably mild
When he went forth in his clothes
Tears of his mother had spent
She sowed with her leaping woe

And the rage of her bloody rent.
Bare of the garments reft
In the costume of water he went
Crushed by the sacrament

Of the heavy blood he had lent.
Unbearably mild was the day
A quarreling of bells in the sky
Delicately the fountains gave

The jet of the living waters to eyes.
Forth from all this walked he
In a language foreign to us
Transparently back into earth.

Did we see him or think we did
Back from his jaunting journey
To the keep and its dark plot early?
Heartbreakingly mild the day

A mystery of flowers in the sky . . .

II
O where is that mirth and furore
Worked by his casting lords
When he paced the shift of the sea cold side
In his mirage-beholding blood?

Nothing that did not have a voice
In the coils of his veins and salt
When he wound forth like a sailor crooked
By a snail-backed hump of net

And unraveled his whole soul's pack
Down the winding thread to the knot
By patched and knit and unknit web
To skein all origin out.

Or strapped to wings when he went
To call his towers in a cloud
Nothing but did not there abound
In the dissembling element

When Merlin of sails and Perseus
On a beast's back he stood and struck,
Ghost-sieging kiss and lineament
By rack and rein and line to get

For an emblem in a shroud.
O where is that mirth and furore?
Let the birds hush and the clouds stop
Their restless building on battlements

That we saw him drawn down
By the water-doused and wind-shaking dark—
Agape birds by his trident cries—
To the musing source where he lies.

III
Unbearably mild was the day
When he went forth in his clothes.
In the foreign skies of our flowers
The headlong bells bay out.

A panging of bells in the wind
For the one death over again
And clouds that the birds run to
From the sky that the bells tear out.

Bear bells your grief away
Bear bells that breaking bay
When he went forth in his mother's clothes
In the leap of tears to the vault.

Bear bells that cracked love bolt
Forth on water and light
To drive with the birds and the cloudshot towers
Through the gay transfiguring night.

A Figure for J. V. Meer

She who weighs pearls, who plays lutes
By the crimson rug on a table,
By the chair with lions reared on its back
Standing, posed, facing the full fall of light
There over her left shoulder,
Or interrupted at music, or clasping a book
In a yellow jacket bordered by ermine,
Or in a blue robe, leaves far voluted the color of blue
In her hair,
In her hand the slender gold trumpet,
By a sloping dish, a peach divided in half,
By the spinet marbled in brown, gray, and black,
Gray and gold the checkerwork of the floor,
Stilled standing there in a mesh
Of the movement of light on light
As fixed it would genuflect
On the studs of the chair,
On a pearl in the ear,
Silks on the wall, maps, ewers, and globes
And waiting stilled there
Lifting up to the eyes of the server
Mouth bemused, a sweetness resting there
As if from some inward air,
Steps in the soul or what
All attention must bend to hear
Bliss like a tempering messenger . . .

And the blue velvet chair, the spinet or virginals,
The letter, a wineglass that covers the mouth,
The viola upon its back and a lute
On the page of music by the gilt frame—
Allusions and scriptless emblems
Like the fish or the peacock or vine,
Signs for the ungiven thing
She converses with on that light gathering in.

And whoever she is standing there
About to play music or hear
From that server who bears foretellingly
Measures into a chamber
The clairvoyance of lemon made northern by amber,
A sense of some brimming raised in a cup . . .
As if deep back in the interior
Enclosed by the coffered rim
Gildings from the illuminations,
Figures in gold-leaf flame,
Returned through translucence again
Atomies of the passion,
A vial of roses and blood.
Like a clarity of being become
A concordance, an equation, this light
With the soul transformed in its chamber.

A Demon Came to Me

A demon came to me in love's disguise,
One of the lower order of hell's guard,
The devil's angel, as it once was coined,
Cool as marble, with a heart like iron.
I could not see it then, the demon smiled
And past experience warned but would not prove.
Besides, the fellow was so very proud,
Immaculate in blackness like a god,
And rife with Adam's ruddy vainglory.
This angel, arrogant of life, swore love.
I, casting off the weight of my short past,
Swore truth was half in novelty's red chance,
And thus in his squat cage I basked.
Foul was fair and fair was foul, confess!
To such confusion have I paid betimes.
Who loves his demon fears his life,
Who loves his pain denies his god.

Incantatory Poem

Hearing that you would come who by my love
Have dreamed me into your head these lost long days
I have caught birds and freed their essential blaze
For still I am as always my heart's hungering slave
And thus but dream life into its beat form
Singing up voices out of the wine-gay blood.

Water and wine being the elements
I was big with cliffs and water-wracking rocks
And huger than I my heart hearing your own
Racing thus to come nearest home with cloud
Under its rain-bearing leaves that were your name
Meaning waif of the tribe of cloud and rain,
Hearing that you would come, blood climbed on bone.

Hearing that you would come in the green cold days
Neither good nor great, my wine-flown blood
Got up incanting sleep's towers to the moon
To pray she bring her sailing presence round
From the back of night that she flag you home
(And dry brook beds she rushes into sound)
Lest all be storm-blown out to deeps
Raging beyond your name, and you not come
By spring's first fields already clad
To herald your long ride down.

By spring's first fields where the darkness there
Rose up to put your wild warmth on
Till absence shaped your body by absence learned
On the pitch of dark to light at my very hand
Under whose pulse you lay where my shaking heart
By its long stroke got you out of sleep
Into dream's childing origins.
Your name wearing water in cloud and flame
The world bearing flowers out of your name

Or in the dim sleep nothing borne
But the sound of waters racing your blood
And the running of waters and the dim
Bemused confession of waters foretelling your coming,

Bearing in morning over the threshold
South-infused, storm-centered, surly,
Purely peace-seeking as the rose
Till wonder lay waking at the heart early
Hearing that you would come for whom by my love
Bells and their tongues wait,
Birds in the bell of the bush their small songs halt.

Hearing that you would come
By the waters charged with your traveling home
On the speed of the surf-worked spume,
I make a prayer I shape upon a poem
Cut from the essential dealers of the green,
Too long dissembled from the water-swearing birds
And make a poem I shape upon a prayer
To this all-fathering dark now come to flower
When day was broken and we lie
Crossed with birds out of your name
I stole by watches of the griefless dream
In the element of the wine-transfiguring world.

The Land We Did Not Know

With what fond ignorance we came
To all that land that did not know we were
Which cared not if we lay upon its downs
And took our worship for the thing it had
From all eyes passing by that way.
It takes more ignorance than the heart can say
To stare as we did at each tree and stone
As if we'd found a world unknown
When gravestone upon gravestone in the wood
Has lost its names and half its words
In the dark avalanche of snows and dews
And all the rains and pickings of the birds.

It takes such passion as the ignorant know
Who out to save that folly, tell the dead,
Tell books and history, ignorance is delight—
As if it were! And yet to keep pitch pure
Must hope to know the thing unknown
As if both they and it had just begun—
Which only can be reached to through those eyes
And hungered lips that measured out the scope
And gave to each bird kin and each stone name
In the felicitous unity all would make.

The passion is to keep the ignorance up
Till wonder gets so saturate with the thing not known
You have become the thing you knew by loving most
What most compels us to the land's beginning.
And thus, my upland slope, I touch you here
Incredulously, like one who comes
To greet you, walking on the tiptops of the trees.

Catch What You Can

The thing to do is try for that sweet skin
One gets by staying deep inside a thing.
The image that I have is that of fruit—
The stone within the plum or some such pith
As keeps the slender sphere both firm and sound.

Stay with me, mountain flowers I saw
And battering moth against a wind-dark rock,
Stay with me till you build me all around
The honey and the clove I thought to taste
If lingering long enough I lived and got
Your intangible wild essence in my heart.
And whether that's by sight or thought
Or staying deep inside an aerial shed
Till imagination makes the heart-leaf vine
Out of damned bald rock, I cannot guess.
The game is worth the candle if there's flame.

My Frantic Heart

My frantic heart awoke
In the middle of the night.
What foot trod the stairs?
Who sobbed below in the street?
The crawling silence told
Nothing, and my loud heart shrieked.

The image of the sufferer
Abides at every street.
These mourning crowds at noon
Numb to their exit, break
For entrance that has no retreat.
The concrete and the buildings sink
Imagination to a terrible use.
Our passion wastes against a vile produce.

Such darkness falls from day
How may you and I and they
Endure enschooled reality?
No taxi stops to let you out
No foot is running on the stair
And all forgiven, all forgot,
That makes you and redemption what
Frees a whole society
From the death that it knows not.

Their living death is in my heart.

And you, my only one, who've gone
And return not, nor will,
The image of your stricken face is they
And I am crying in the street miles away.

This Swallows' Empire

Wrought by the odd desire for permanence
I'd hammer down that barn's boards one by one
The ivy's nudged apart and winds have sprung
And icy blows and summer's pounding suns.
Those gaping windows, too, and half-cracked panes,
The door that broke from its hinges leans against
The blackened exit mouth, and all such things
As let the rude rot in and thieving rain
I'd be so prompt to take defense against
And fortify and make so sound
You'd think it'd haunt me on some howling night
When all seems waste unless I could
To all that trouble say: this much will stand,
This swallows' empire for a little while
And bolts of hay in their warm cave
And drifts of straw upon the broad-beamed floor.
Though time must turn all waters for its mill
And nothing is but grist as we well know
What has withstood two hundred years
That rich resistance will do so
If obdurate work allows, for fifty more
For fifty more to house the hay
They cut and piled in stripèd rows
And will carry in before the sun's flower goes.

As if within this shelter here
For what the toppling wagons bring
From ricks in fields to fill the loft
With rustling fragrance and with warmth
There might be some more delicate thing
Dozing as in some attic in some spring
That shafts in through the windows in a dream
Of meadows in their prime unreaped, uncut,
Unreaped, uncut, and running with the wind—
The golden burn, the darksome gold or green.

Pressed to the rafters all that airy weight
And caught within, now looking out,
Past time's compulsions in the massy dark,
Their golden heads and stalks of light.
I mean those summers of the foursquare fields
That memory by its strange persuasion yields,
And blazoning, from dim abandonment.

For the Fountains and Fountaineers of Villa d'Este

Say that these are the fireworks of water,
One hundred fountains on the tiers of plains;
That goddesses enthroned hold spears of it,
It erupts from the mouths of shagged eagles,
And moss-legged gods, one side of the face worn off by it,
Straddle the silver, unmitigated flood.
Say that the down play and up play
And fourteen shafts around a central plume
Not to discount the dragons spouting it
That meet two dolphins plunged in it
Sending their streams against the contending ones,
Are a continuum in a series of play by water
And play by light on the water, making arcs
Of a spectrum in the din and bafflement
Of that most muffled watery bell beat, pell mell and lulled stampede,
So that an insatiable thirst
Cannot be allayed in the blood.
Though they flow round the very bones,
Though a tumult of vapor rising from them
Blows the leaves of the tree by their weight,
Nothing, no, not by any rain-making vows
Nor any meandering of boughs
Down the stone-flagged paths and the avenues
Of the serpentine oleander
Whose branch knots and slippering leaves
Knit such a shade in the place of green light
It is a scandal of pleasure,
Say that nothing, no limestone grotto alive
With the sibylline god gushing forth
This silver, non-potable liquid,
Can convey to the fever coolness
Nor a slaking, a quenching by dews
Where the scent of the water buds.

Here are fans of water, and silver combs,
Peacock-eyed in the sun-glints upon them,
Vines and wreaths trailed round a stone,
And thirst has become delirium,
It heaps on the brain,
It plunges along the arm,
In a sleep by leaves
It buries half the blood.
Taking one sinuous course down the breast
It would thrust and lock round the heart in a trice.

While, to stand, sheathed in a grotto
On the reverse side of this shield of water,
Downpouring in pound on pound
Its chafed, silver-shot metal . . .
I know of no fury that tells
More to me, deafening, than that
Of a velocity past which I'd know
Nothing but the hurl and fall
Of those burst rockets of water
Driving their sweetness into the ground
In a blaze of lightnings and stars
As in wet dusts shattering on stone
To explode with soft fury again.

Shield of the water and water wall,
Water roots, tentacles, bars,
Spears of water and bolts,
I know nothing here but the sense
In this downflowing fall
Of the wilderness of eternity.
And I am flailed to earth.
I am dank as a river god.
Scallop on scallop of the primeval flat water leaf

With no roots but in water, taking its substance from liquid,
Coats me and jackets me over.
I am dense as lichen,
Primordial as fern,
Or, like that tree split at its base,
Covert for winter creatures and water-retreated life,
Tip with my boughs very serpent green,
Or in a grand spirit of play
Spurt water out of my nostrils.

Veins and gaddings of water,
I have seen you in a fall
Shoot madness into a marble,
And ever the thud and *pronk* of the pump,
Hee-haw and frog *harrumph!* that heave and rail
Of the mechanical works
That create the genius of water flowing . . .

To tread the crests of the fountains,
To walk on the foam of their flowers,
Upthrust in a vertical climbing
Spires of the falling and changing stuff
In a ghost play of dance
Creating beyond their climbing
Caps of their vapor, a white turbulence
Of that which so changes beyond them
It is sur-foam, surf-combed,
It is got by the mathematics of climbing—
To reach by those aerobatics into white snows of the mounting—
There to dissolve into
What brings all the condensed fury of dews
Back down into descending.

To dance on those heavy heads of water
So richly and artfully sustained

By white prongs and tongues of the air
Curdling up liquid from nowhere,
The advance and the sword of a watery swirl
That is somehow compact with air,
Or to take from the lull
Of the deep music such a dream
As will not abandon flame,
To sink into the deep-blown
Horn-called music and the wind-
Flung and cheek-puffed
Surge and hee-ho-hum of the thing. . .
Shagged eagles that do not spout
By *fleur de lys,* all moss, that do,
And the shafts then and the boat-shaped urn—
Three kinds of shapes of water flowing
Across two kinds of spouts descending
And one out of the mouths of horned or big-eared animal gods.

A water walk by all this bewildering
Fantasy of arising and falling flutes of the water,
Columned water adorned, making a gush and warble of sound.

II

Fountains, if to behold you
Were to have rain down over me
The least tendril and slightest shoot
Of your very white jubilation!
In the coil of your spirits be wound!
Or wrapped in your sleek skins
Mortality itself unfitted,
Made wild as it was, bound in rings
Of the lightly springing-up streams
That go in a series of crystal hoops
And twenty such hoops you have,
Twenty wickets of running light

In glittering slivers of it
Set in an *Alice* water garden
Where the cultivation is water, not earth,
Stamens and stems of water stuff,
Emblems of water pouring from emblems,
Griffons that jut it, like merry she-gods
Winged at the back but firm fish-tailed
From whose breasts spurt the magnificent jets!

As I beheld you down levels of grass,
Throwing out the wild mists of forgetfulness.
Gashing down through the tender grace
Of a green confinement by slopes.
White channels were a most beautiful thing,
Channels, chalk white, with the sluice's spume
Were a most beautiful, astonishing thing
Coursing with mad dog race down the grass
From one fountainous place to the next.
As I saw you in bird-frail seines
Down a green depth of height.
Sinews and locks fine as veils
Showing all vegetation behind them,
Chains, flashing and weaving,
Strands as of links of snow
Released and transformed into air.
Below, a deep chasm, a tangled abyss
Only a bird may sift, flying down the crevasse
For a sip from a luminous beam.

(Are there not butterflies for these surf-flowers?
Do not tell me that one ever drowned
Lingering too long by the gust of some fountain,
Or that those twinkling in teams, parting and closing
The light-dotted vanes of their wings

Ever capsized, riding over a stream
The way song soaring rides down a wind.)

Fountains, our volatile kin,
Coursing as courses the blood,
For we are more water than earth
And less flesh than a flame
Bedded in air and run by the wind—
Bequeath me, be with me, endow my hunger
With sweet animal nature,
Knit me in with the plumes and wands of your favor,
Get me great vistas, jade-milky streams
Where the source of the fury starts,
Winking up the last supper of light.
Get me chrysanthemums, great bulky heads,
And a stem narrow as mercury
Fit to support a bluet.
And out of the reflections of water on stone
Let me count the great arcs,
The clusters rounded as grapes
Or staccato as needles,
All that momentum kept firm
Propelled by the dry force of form—
To rest, momentarily at least
In the cataract of time—
Leaves for his feathers on the breast of an eagle,
Deep light of the long nights and years!

III
In this tranquil life such as belongs to windmills
Though the subtle day does not blow
But stands tranced in the wickets
And aspirations of water,
Descend by these paths, these perspectives,

This cascade of steps by the balustrades
Downgliding as if molded out of waves,
Into the white strata and springs
Of the founding place and wedding of waters.
But you must thrice interpret to know,
Mad on the waters, what they vow. . . .
Listen. The fine battery of them.
Like a purification of sound
Blows their deep chanting,
That murmurous persisting.
No wilier song from the moon
Ever plunged into and took apart,
Dividing the plangent strands of it,
Such a fine cornucopia of bloom.

Like a low meditation on song
Before that song has begun,
This speech over you in a mesh,
This chain-mail of running light and of breath,
This tissue as if of sleep
That is so lightly woven
The dream stares through with its Bacchic locks
Till you hear the very cloth of dream at last
Of figured and intertwined emblems.
Walks in long arches under it,
Portals through which if you go
You are into the white-woven web held fast.
But you must thrice interpret to tell
What is said by a flower in a spell,
Ascending the steps to the gods . . .
You may see them among the flowers,
Standing small-headed, vast-eyed,
The grace of the broad breast turned,
A beardful of weeds and small ones
Lurked there by the marble-veined sides.

And you have gone the ways of each sense
To dam up thirst or to stanch it.
There was a wild stream lashed to a tree
Gave out its oracular oratory.
By a flume came thrasonical volley
Boasting of love and struggle.
Through watery walls blown asunder,
So light the small threads of structure,
By so many gadding ways of the senses
Harnessed to water, knowing what fire
Must make their divine toil turn wheels
For the relentless mills and wills
You came from the watery furnaces,
From springs sealed of the sleep
Smoldering with what divinations
If such may arise and wake.

And meanwhile they stand there, they linger,
They recline, they preside, in languor or rigors,
Gods, our great friends of love and rage.
Passion stares into their empty eyes
Want sees the calm sweet water coursing,
Artfully held in their mouths and pulsing,
Blind waters tranquilly stemming there.

Country without Maps

(1964)

Cortège for Colette

(The Palais-Royal Gardens)

Minister of birds,
Keeper of islands and pools
Where they sink and go down in races
By the mosses and deep scattered sedges,
Collector of grasses, seed-heavy and bent,
Seed of the fern and the violet,
(Known to the moonmen and the green fever),
All receipts and brews, felicitous cures
Under sinewy roofs and streets of the root.

Genius, moreover, of gardens,
The bowknot, the crescent, and square,
And as many circular knots, and that pruning art
The shears do so well with the snail,
Tender and trainer of fountains,
Benefactor of boxwood, quincunx, and yew,
Mathematician of the parterres
By a lapful of sparrows,

I have heard, I have come by these arches and urns,
All the classical battery of forms
Through the rectangular perspectives
Down the long galleries that end in the windows.
Closed are the gates. The calm is great
In the dark, where the small waters blow.
There is a sudden sense of a slow sailing out
As a sudden wind tries a few leaves.
A part of a cloud interrupts the passage
Of the knobbed moon.

And I do not think the garden is what it was.
Like a promise departed, the rectangular perspectives
Down the long galleries end in the windows,

75

Stop with the shutters.
Should I speak I would not be heard
There where the moon slowly sails on,
For where might there be another speech
Such as signs give, and omens,
Such as sense has in those dreams
For which there is no translation except
In the absolutely unheard music about, perhaps, to be given,
Like a part of the secret sky broken off
Just at the surface where it crowds
With those vaguely summoned to take the long turns of the dance?

But let me not, standing outside these gardens,
These oblong gardens, this file of trees
Subject in dark to a murmur of days
Held echoing under their leaves,
Where only some sliver of water sighs,
Spilling over and over into its pool,
Where under the yellow light of the lamps
Only a cat walks, it is late for the arcades
Out of the gardens to keep their own life,
And for low doors opening into mossed courts,
Let me not, to the diminished perspectives
Hovered with ivy where an urn sits, declare
That a part of the world having gone back into itself,
A meaning is thereby lost,
The disappearance of which torments us,
For it was not subtle but gross.
Amidst all this matching of flowers and shapes,
This tending of borders, this cutting by trowels,
Though compelled to pay close attention and not to walk blindly
As if in a massacre of petals,

To know
That that of which you were the great witness lives,

That the torn butterfly will not leave the page,
Pierced by the light you gave,
That by the power not to forget
Profoundly connecting with the root
You brought by its weight some perfected whole
Of a part of the self into flower,
Who lightly go to the grave,
Having expended all you could give.

Nor to speak of the corruption of ivy
Nor of absence where presence dwells
Nor of darkness where there is love.
To be mute, to be mute about death,
To address the invisibles
For whom your genius, like a delicate beast
Training your heart,
To your sense giving lessons,
Led you out of the one world
Into how many nuages—embarkings!

And simply to lift up the flower,
Simply to salute the cloud,
From the cat to the horse by way of the dragon,
To some striped sky by way of the bird
That it be borne, your body,
In the arms of young men round and round
And to the march blown by bugles
That the dark iron of its velvet vow
Shock through the blood some understanding
Just as sensory as perfume when the touched body
Gives forth the divine humors of rain and leaves.

Amsterdam Letter

Brick distinguishes this country,
And broad windows—rather, rectangles
Of wide and glittering scope—
And cabbages.
Cattle a specialty, and cheese, storks—if they are not all dead
Or abandoned—and flowers, oh, flowers!
Some say as well, quick humor.
Is it a specimen of humor that a cabdriver proposes to marry me?
The speaking of English is at least general.
Also I have spoken a little Dutch with an old Frisian lady.
How affable she was, amusing and helpful!
(They *are* helpful and affable, and their far too occasional teams of
    horses
Wear rosettes by the ears.)
Aside from that, and above all, the dense, heavy, fragrant sky
And rich water, a further extension of color—
The sky a low window over this twining of green water and
    bridges—
And the sedate, gabled houses pressed closely together
And bicyclists, six abreast or more,
Skimming round corners like swallows.
How quiet they are! even the trolleys!
While the trains seem to glide like sleighs on runners
So that after those many places dedicated, it would seem, to clatter
The absence of it becomes an active delight in itself.

The delight is in part, of course, the lovely dividing of the city
By those ancient and ripe-green canals, and the mixed fragrance
Of the River Amstel and roasting coffee,
And the bravura of carved animal heads, the elegance of panels,
And those panes of violet and panes flushed yellow
That alternate the clear meaning of glass
With the blindness of shutters closed over warehouse windows,

And that Gothic German French sense of the arabesque and the
    scroll,
The urn and the garland of leaves.

As for that delicacy of manner, that responsiveness to many,
That prevalence of what seems self-possessed, contained, and easy—
I am speaking of those who went out of their way
To lead me to Rembrandt's house
(Which in his lifetime he lost),
Of the woman at the Cantine,
Of the Madame, too, in the Zeedjik,
Amiable conversationalists
Who did not make me feel stupid
Because I would never speak their language,
Who by a manner suggested
What I have no word for—
Unfeigned it is and unblighted,
That "generous, free disposition"
That so strongly confirms
A fitness of things,
As do also the upright geraniums,
All of which, by the elm-dark canals
(Where dogs on the loose loped up to me
With cold, wet noses
And ducks paddled under the Seven Arches
And the gilt swan rode on the crest of the fortified tower),
Offered some measurable glimpse of what
There, by the water beds
And the ancient, calmed passions of their reflections,
Informed me as the moon does,
Which was in part the pleasure of learning
Those words that I did from the old Frisian woman—
Horse, sky, cow, tree, thank you, I mean,
Beauty, and love.

Invitation to a Hay

A settlement of love
Is what I'd risk if you would.
A central fountain and a horse,
A little native elegance,
Some green-shuttered saffron buildings
And avenues of leaning trees
And an orchard close by
Divided from a field of hay
By a mouldering old wall
Snaking up a hill.
I'd have a garden primed
With beanflowers and chick peas
And in tubs lemon trees
Not to forget the marveled orange—
Where is a fruit so bright
And a stem so delicate?—
And days of blue air
That crowd the dark boughs of a grove
And other days as pale
As light in a birch grove—
Oh birch my very white
And original delight!
And back of us and all around
For the castle-haunting rooks
To fly to and fro from
The many-sided, dark-blue faced
Mountains, wrinkled, ravined, cleft
When they are not cast upon
By those pallors that beyond
Tell of a snowlight's origin.
And in this civil order
Ringed round by a wilderness
I'd have some very conical
And shaggy house of hay
To invite you in to stay

As long as butter-yellow walls pleased you
And there you'd be with me
We'd live in a monument of hay
Mad as those who know
In love is all fantasy.
Your breast would be of burning gold
And its delicious heat
Would warm me day and night
While creatures of the wood
Might envy, if they could,
Our joy just as fine
As the improvising clouds
That as you look at them are gone
Or volatile as leaves in wind.
We'd go bird-nesting in clouds
And hunting down the meadow grass
For flowers or the smallest haunts
Of the young field mice.
And in this ancient landscape
Preponderant with moss,
Rambling walls and pinewoods
Of narrow alleys at the end of which
Daylight stares starkly through,
Our love alone would be new
Despite its ancient properties.
Aërial would we be
With love's finest courtesies,
By all that shapes of earth and air
Can subtilize the senses with
Until they have grown rapt
On emanations of a light
When fold on fold goes into
Five fathoms of a blue.
Our love would be endowed
By mountain and by cloud

So long as we would stay
Alongside such ravines
And such slopes of terraced vines
Broken towers and bells
In a shaggy house of hay.
My dear, and will you be
Content to dwell with me
Eating of illusion
Daily and nightly?

Last Letter to the Scholar

Come, lecturer on love, resume your rostrum.
Preach to the mad dead roses of the year.
Preach to my heart that's buried in the garden
Under the yellowed petals since you left.
Though deaf by those haranguing winds
The winter plagues dead petals with, and leaves
Long fluttering upon the barren ground or straying
Around the broken stems and shackled thorns,
Your voice by its compelling sweetness will
Spring to winter bring, and numb roots start
Alive to pierce and quick the dark
That closed around with killing cold what heart
I had, after you'd come and left.

My dear, you'll call this fallacy
Pretentious, or some fustian idiocy
To claim my ticking heart was put from me
Into some troped-up garden of old rue.
Forgive, because I set up roses too,
Improbable as madrigals. And chide
My errant language that would claim
I died, or nearly died, for loss of you.
Chide, but believe. I live, but I am dead.
But that's not what I mean. Who lives
Must learn to live his deaths. Who loves
Must learn the same. We blaze and char
As love is near or far
In that small world that's ordered to our want
But likewise bounded by love's eyes and lips.
The expanded world thus so contracted, what
Fires that come consume us when they're out.
And death's more amorous than not
And just as subtle sudden and chameleon cruel.

So preach to me, and tell me less of death
Than love that outlasts death, as I've heard tell.
Tell me that my heart confined
And sunken low within the flesh's earth
Will, when you come again, awake
And know its Easter in your sight
As may those thwarted roses rise
Some later on to your rare light
Compounded of much heat and spirit.
Tell me that this death's not long.
Be hortatory, admonitory, and calm
In your bright fever, that the clear estate
The world is when you're here will get again
Its lease to be, as you propound
How to our destiny we grow as one
If two, with such split hearts as we own,
Not sanguined by experience, may so dream
An absolution clement as the rain.

Spring Song II

And now my spring beauties,
Things of the earth,
Beetles, shards and wings of moth
And snail houses left
From last summer's wreck,
Now spring smoke
Of the burned dead leaves
And veils of the scent
Of some secret plant,

Come, my beauties, teach me,
Let me have your wild surprise,
Yes, and tell me on my knees
Of your new life.

"Thy Love Is One Thou'st Not Yet Known"

Let us be quiet today. The earth is still,
The sun is drowsy, sleeping in the clouds
Like sleepless birds of day who take to rest
Or take at least to silence in their nests
Only some very few adventured out
To stride the levels of the rusty grass.

But for the crickets in a singsong shrill
Of notes too small to be called notes,
Some tick and jilt of quaver in the low tangle
Soprano as some fifing of an elf
Or other hopping creatures made of green,
Green-whiskered, green-antennaed, green-armored,
There is no other cry or breath.
                                        Air is still
As every flower tells and every leaf,
And waters where they were subside to wells
Or sink their resourceful chatter underground.

As if the quick of all that stir and bloom
By brook and wind commotion, ceaseless play
Of clouds, leaves, action of the plants
That in their beds stand taller every day
Had taken a quietus or, quiescent,
Retired into some first most voiceless place
Begot by silence on a stillness,
An in-going into the unlustred zone
Of some more hermit energy
That gets the tendrils of the sense
Their dwelling place in a white hush

And makes the instant finer than a dream.
But is not dream but rather's known
By burning fineness of a light

More lucid than the air and only sensed
In violent wide-awakeness on a cloud.
Only by the raveling of such bonds
As strips the day to garments of the flower—
To leaning lilies much too tall
To sustain their flaring crowns,
Veronica, vervain, bent over by the rain,
And Queen Anne's lace upon its gawky stem.

A Note to La Fontaine

I have come into the time of the ant.
The grasshoppers are bitterly paying.
Their fiddles are broken, they are lame and laid up,
The ants are sneering: "Now dance!"
And the grasshoppers, in an ague of shivering,
Faint for a morsel, seem to be trying.
It is not good to see. How may I have this tribe starve?
It is a slap in the face of all I believe
To concede that the sour ones, safe in their barracks
Where they so promiscuously scurry,
Should have every right to be dry and ironic.
Survival is *not* the test, and is a long life the best?
Fie on the righteous dullards
So proud of their sweltering summer labor
That allows them to live without honor through winter.
The grasshoppers have more grace
Than to make out for themselves any case.
With that knowledge they'll die
Spitting into the bleak eye
Of those who never had such song
To make life seem dancing and warm.

Epitaph for My Cat

And now my pampered beast
Who hated to be wet,
The rain falls all night
And you are under it.
Who liked to be warm,
Are cold as any stone,
Who kept so clean and neat,
Cast down in the dirt
Of death's filthy sport.

Pays Perdu

There are those days, vivid and pure,
When everything dazzles, new found.
It is on days like this that we understand Eden,
Old worlds of the Golden Hours.
What is it. It is vigor, freshness,
A sense of the flags of day flying free,
It is commodious harmony,
We have fallen into some deepest relation
With self, the sense, and the world,
We are at rest strenuously
For all has form, moves with vivacious fluidity.
Then—nothing that seems extraneous
From the voices of bells caught, parted and cast away
To the blazings of twenty butterflies
Bemused on a stalk of blue flowers.
As if we had composed the day
With the sleeping unseen at the back of the mind
And we neither faint nor pale.
'When we are happy we have other names.'

So it was on that day in the country
When my friend and I at large in a town
Fortified on its rock above a green river
(A champing and nervous force that had cut
Whole landscapes in two in its glacier course)
Started out at the height of noon
On the broad footpath by the river
Past gardens of garlic and artichoke
And groves of olive established in tiers.
It was in Provence and by the Var
In a country of vineyards and lizards
And the fragrance of many rough herbs in bloom,
St. John's Eve, almost, and yet not come,
The perfect summer essence of the year.
Now, as we were along the way

We stopped to talk to a passerby
Proud to dispense the lore of the country,
A stranger herself, who spoke of a village
Far down the way, by the river, and of another
Far up in the mountains, hard if not impossible to find,
From which donkeys came down twice a week,
There being no road but a donkey track
And this track its only link with the world.
She herself had seen neither one
But she liked to think of them lurking
At the end of some straggling path. So did we,
And following her vague suggestion
That the one called Lacs, up in the mountains,
Was somewhere *down* and then *up*, set out,
Larky and confident.

This much we knew, that in an old country
That holds many bones, where life has been hard,
Where much dust of the nightingales
Is mixed with the dust of poppies
And the stubborn roots of valerian, and all
The medicinal sages
That in an old country crossed by centuries of animals and men
There are many paths possible to take.
Foxes and dogs made them first,
Horses and donkeys succeeded.

Then the paths were secured, steps were cut out,
Walls were erected.
An old country is criss-crossed with paths,
Short cuts to the crest of a mountain.
Look at some track up the terraces
Where the olive trees doze
And you ought to know it is going somewhere.
We took one on some such faith.

II

And of the three-hour walk in the blaze of day
Up the snail-spiralling way of the rough country—
Scrub-oak and stone—
And the three vertigoes when the path fell sheer
By the cliffside straight to the river
And there was white limestone dust and a chalky glare
Blinding—
                    and the heat—till we cooked—
And knew the beginnings of thirst—
                                                        and were lost

Or deceived by a choice of paths
So retraced our steps to a farm
And the goat-faced owner who had been asleep
Shouting down from the upper story window
(After his dogs had barked themselves hoarse)
That if we wanted to visit a *pays perdu*
Take the fork back there to the left—

And of the way up by hawk's beak and claw
By rock horn and fang and skull,
By the death's head grin of the spurred headlands
As the path twisted inland
Broad enough at times for two donkeys
But losing us in the basil and marjolain
And long ceased the groves of the flickering olive,
The derelict houses and storing sheds
As we climbed on past a pine wood,
The sun glinting on their tufts and their cones
And baking the rock formations.
And into what were we going, leaving the river,
That broad boulevard, that viable thread,
To go back and into the crowded interior,
Crowded, that is, with trees and more rock and many small
    mountains

That engendered, for all that we knew, cockatrices. . . .
And at one turning in a medley of rubble
Meeting a child, a little girl,
Carrying a basket that had a cloth cover
Who was so startled on seeing us and hearing us speak
That we thought her a mute, she taking so long to answer
And then in a voice as if rusty from long disuse.

This was the first stage: after that, more declivities,
More mournful ostentation of stone as we climbed
And knew thirst and passed through more deadlands
Meeting the sense of the torture of time.
History is time and it assailed us, the sight of those signs of that static
    tempest that had once pressed forth those needles of rock that
    once again met us, and the swirled water-marked rippled bad-rock
    effects across yet another harsh breach in earth's crust cut by the
    Var's tributary

And if music is the energy of time, immensely loading some quarter-
    hour with the compressed violence of meanings too numerous,
    shades too elusive striving against the iron gates and in one crazed
    hurl achieving the leap, so the ever continuing variations of new
    fantasies of rock made us laggard. Impressed us? Oppressed us.
Ejaculations of rock pipes with crumbling flutings! Perches for birds
    or stylites, grotesque and badly botched Byzantine pillars!

And our weak shoes half in ribbons from so much pulverizing by
    pebbles.
And we streaked with sweat and the taste of much dryness in the
    mouth.
Grown over by land, by what we had seen,
Bruised by the stones white with dust and pollen,
Burnt by the sun in a mirth
Of the incurable singing of the nightingale.
For we had spied on the bird in a round bush

Though that was below, near the river.
Up here, in the miles inward, bees followed us
But not that Greek thrush. Here it was birdless,
Wildness in waste.
And the disintegrating black schist,
Porphyry headlands, beetling and angled . . .

And then, by a turn, roofs!
And our drouth drank of the cordial.
For here would be the douce water, casks of it, vats,
And we dreamed up the *café,* for what town was without one,
Where we would sit, steeped in mineral water.
Citron pressé, and after that *café*
Before we'd begin on water again.

But as a mountain is never the same
When you are traveling toward it,
Presenting at each turn another view of its one hundred faces
And as space itself is as deceiving,
So we lost that prospect, another turning swallowed it up,
We jogged on, thinking of donkeys
And what sort of people were those who lived so far inland?
And who could ever take over these mountains?
Dense earth resisted, hail to its lordship
That would thrust us out of its holdings!

Nor by more turnings did the roofs swim back
Although we came to a bridge
Where the path broadened into a road.
Now the sky was staring with a sudden stark blue
Over the flank of a new mountain
And two or three paths coiled before us.
All was less wild, we had modulated
Into what might have been at one time subdued
By the plough, though forgotten by now,

A table of land half pasture,
And we went this way and that
Attempting to skirt the shape of the land.
Was it a mirage? We half joked.
Had our thirst started up a fever so soon?
Wasn't it an hour ago we had seen
The tiptilting roofs? Into what had they gone?

Then suddenly a wheatfield
And a lane or a gully of stones and a sharp hill
Up which we stumbled into storm blue,
The sky full of violent, crazed blue,
And a wind rolling in the trees
By a haycock shaped like a loaf of bread
And truly the roofs and surely the water!
And we running now across the shorn field
Till we came to the first faces of houses.
The field rode up to their windows
And the shutters on them were closed
And the silence could not be more unstirred
Until we called out and black and white doves
Started up with a creak of wings
And we called again. But where were the people?
Was it inhabited by black and white doves or pigeons?

III

And we went around a corner, if you can call it that, between one
    house with its roof fallen in and one whole one and came into a
    courtyard with lime trees in bloom and three or four houses across
    the way and saw a woman wearing a man's peaked hat and a
    man's shoes running with a pack of hay on her back and a woman
    in a big straw hat and three dogs that came at us snarling and as
    the wind buffeted the lime trees and the crazed blue grew stal-
    wart we saw *this* was the town but *there* was the water running
    from a pipe's mouth into a tub. What a stir! for if we were appari-

95

tions to them they were not less to us, and the dogs barking for all
they were worth till a man called them off and one who had been
willing to hurl himself at our throats now wagging his tail as we
explained how long we had been walking and—THIRST! And he
pointed triumphantly at what they had an abundance of.

Then we rather crazy there at the tub, filling our hands with water.
And my friend lying prone and drinking from the pipe's mouth . . .
While bundles of hay kept flying past us on the backs of the man
    and woman and the one in a straw hat calling out to them in a
    language we had never heard to which was added the delirium
    of birds just before rain—swallows springing out of nowhere to
    shriek and to skirl and a swooping of pigeons while a battery of
    crows cawed by.

And as the storm sky humped down I running out in the unearthly
    blue to the 'other side' of the town . . . which was likewise a field
    that stretched off to a mountain. But more. Much more. Where I
    stood was before the very birth of a chaos of definable forms.
So here they were, put down in a lull, the last lull between peaks.
Since to the 'back' or the 'north' stretched that beginning of the one
    thousand wrinkled circus-net tops.

Till the rain came down in a blithe bluster of spears and the air was
    so freshened with the breath of all that seems good that the rain
    froze and we were peppered with a fine shot of hail and took
    refuge under a shed until the man who had been carrying hay
    asked us into his house.

And we saw, going in, a bright blue postbox at the side of his door.

And we went into the first black room
Filled with blossoms of the lime tree in gunny sacks
And loose on the floor and on a table, and into the kitchen
With an iron stove and scraps in a pan on the floor for a dog

And the woman in the peaked hat was there
With eyes that ate up her face
Nodding to us and smiling but sitting away where we could not
    see her,
Sitting away in a corner like a bird mewed up,
And her husband eager to do the talking
With the stub of a burnt-out cigarette
In the corner of his mouth like a sore,
Slight and not young,
His beret jammed tight to his head . . .
And he wanted to know just how we had happened to come
Because, where they were, few did
And was it true that the donkeys went down
Twice a week or more? we asked.
About that, he was vague. Yes, he had donkeys
And when the wheat was cut—
We understood then that truly at times
The donkeys went down with produce
And returned with provisions.
And we heard of the postman who came twice a week
Five miles by the ravines and the gorges
Because there was a postbox and it was the law
Whether there was mail or not—
And of a teacher who also came
Twice a week or so for the one child left.
So. They were not forgotten. He voted.
And they had gone to war,
Two families left now, and one child.
And Lacs had been named for a lake
That had disappeared so long ago
Not even his father's grandfather had seen it
And this house—almost as old!
They had sheep till the shepherd had left
And years ago there had been hundreds—
Sheep, that is, with their shepherds

Up from the valley to stay the whole summer.
In his father's day there had been horse roads
Now grown over, and the houses for lizards . . .
He was quick and gentle in the way he spoke
Wearing a cigarette that would not stay lit,
Steadfastly refusing our own.
No animal earth-spirit, weathered and contrary,
But equable, civil,
We felt that it pleased him to talk,
Especially of the heroical postman,
And the thistle hearts that his mother cooked
For the good that it did them;
Like that herb that she swore if you put in your shoe
You could walk miles and never get tired
But he used to walk to the valley half the nights of the week.
Youth was his herb.

And of what else we talked about . . .
As the lime blossoms trembled in the next room
Where a wild bee stumbled and throbbed. . . .
Of the grass fire that made the bees leave
(When they kept bees) and bees won't come back
To a place that's burned
And the mushrooms and snails that came after rain
And one time, long after midnight,
The chapel bell rang and rang
And whether the wind or an animal rang it,
For the rope had worked loose, they never knew.

And the strange Lacs stirred for us
As the lime blossoms trembled in the next room
When he peopled the sides of hill,
Had carts jolting by that took wheat to a mill,
Humors of barnyards, the Gaulois cock crowing,
Goats with their niddering voices, vigor and motion

And all the desires we connect with action
Before the roofs fell and the field mice came in. . . .
And how is it, we wanted to say,
As you gather the lime flowers to store or to sell,
Though it take the whole heart do you labor
So close to the nerve and burn
Of the great stars in the stillness
That is as strong as sound. . . .

While he told of the fete, just at this time of year,
Of John the Baptist when a handful of men
Would go into the mountains to a "desert" there
And stay for two nights, fasting and praying,
And on the night they came back
Everyone going to meet them
With flutes and fifes and the moaning procession . . .
And where the chapel was just over the meadow
And what the woman spoke who wore the straw hat
Was Provençal. . . .

And the rain had long since stopped
And it was time to go
And he would not accept our cigarettes
Though there was the thought we would send him a postcard
If nothing else for the sake of the postman
And we said our farewells and his wife smiled back
With that look not to be pitied nor understood
And out into Lacs again
We saw what we had not seen before—
Two houses stood sound and whole
And the rest toppling like hollyhocks
Or topless, with a tree gushing from a door.
And we saw how secluded and secret,
How inward a crumbling thing looks,
The eyeless ruins or the three-cornered ones.

And time not running away as in music
Nor the instant lit up with energy
But grinding and pulverizing with an idiot's patience
The rock foundations.
And it would not be stopped. It would be
As the wind and the weather would have it,
It would go down to the soundless possession
Of the rash bugles of morning glory.

And what can we do, said my friend,
Can we send them something, a gift.
They have given up, they are dying,
They are going down with the place
And this—she waved her hand
For we were passing the fields again
And the same big pigeons beating up—
Makes them indifferent. They are too much lulled
By the lull in the mountains.
And the fields swelling to the green horns of hills.
It could not be more beautiful
Nor the quality of the way it lay
In between old hills and young mountains
Could not be met again
Nor the sounding of the silence
That we would have in our ears for days.
And we passed the hay rick and found the path
Leaving that phantasmal space
For which once we left it, there could be no maps.
Pays perdu! said the goat-faced man
And *lacs* also meant a snare made with strings
To catch birds with, as we understood.

And who was to say that their souls were held
In the space here in between mountains
As the thyme and the rosemary perfume the shadows

That the great bodies cast down from their crowns?
And who was to speak of mountain flowers
That can blossom only after snow and deep frost,
Their colors intensified by the rare air,
Resisting the aridity, the cold nights, the poverty of soil,
Indeed, these very deprivations, that struggle
Being necessary for their perfection of a few days?
It was not to say this
                                    in the great light
And the forms aloof over the serenity of ruins.

And we took the long way down,
Loping along it easily in the cool of the day,
Not tormented by thirst,
As the small perfumes of earth began to be freed,
The dry-shod ferny gusts,
And shawls of blue shadow cast
On the pale green of dented slopes
Whole peaks in shadow
And whole landscapes in cloud—
"Those intricate thoughts, those elaborate emotions—"
Where at the converging of four peaks
A cloud makes a fifth.

New and
Selected Poems

(1967)

An Improvisation upon the Theme of
The Lady and the Unicorn

(Musée de Cluny)

These are her angels!
Frighten her not with seven heads on a stalk!
They guard her sleep in a parable of flowers,
The plumed porcupine
And he of the great horn in the middle of his head
Who paws with laughing modesty the rose standard
Or in a pavilion wears armorial bearings,
Goat-bearded, his breast broader than day,
Breasting the pennant more white than she
Whose skin sheds light as she bathes white in a pool
Where the flutist blows

By a field of blue upon the rose, rose red
And flowers, her simple flowers, degrees of rose,
Where on the dark blue he of the red stocking'd legs proffers
The small heart split at the top that the fingers hold

And flowers, her simple flowers that print the day,
Her Michael-fighting pennant, rose and gray,
And major beasts and lesser beasts, those winged stags
Exultant as deities, whiteness, her rose,
Over which a pennant emblazoned with three moons
More formal and more salient than the sea
Sails out to greet the swollen-bellied ship
That flaunts with answering streamers in the bay

By this, primavera, in the morning of the year
And by daisies, the arbiters of justice and goodness,
Is she appointed to her destiny,
And the red heart burns like a jewel or a fire,
We are held by the heart as he hands it
Not to be played with or eaten by his lady.
The flowers revolve with the beasts around it
While from the knee joints of armor stare faces

And the lion is clasped by his fetlock,
His spanieled feet and arched tongue flared
Like the backwards foil of the lily.

While the unicorn without pasture or fence
Beholds his face stitched in the glass,
Who white as day lights up dark speech,
Maintaining the lion's valor. Though he looks
In a glass at his image, he need not,
He suffers he singular, needing none other,
Though in the herbage you may see him again,
Reduced in stature.
                    Need not look in the glass
(Being of the glass, lord of the maze and enigma,
Where each thing to its degree
Is beheld in its entity,
Such as Reynard, such as the dove, and the wolf
Fallen headfirst into a trap, and the porcupine
Plumed, it would seem, or his quills supine),
Who is Quintessential,
Toute Belle,
Pursuivant to all that was hunted for,
Who glides inwoven in flowers, himself the pulled thread,
Infinite relations in his train
In the *perceforest* of shadow.
Who gives a scripture to smiling eyes,
To the small mouth that sweetly psalms,
Being all signs and figures of love.

Blood and the whiteness of day,
She of the sole desire, dogs, deer,
Stupendous bear embracing,
The hare that leaps behind a stretched rope
In the season of venery,
Each with his part in the thirsty quest,

Subjects all of the single objective;
Truly they, like the planets, whirl in an earth order!
Truly here, in a fresh candor,
The bather bathes in the parapets of lilies,
And earth bears everywhere the upstanding flower,
Fruit wood with yellow quince clearly,
Clearly in a fresh candor conceived.
The vair-rose trumpet that her Michael blows,
He jams the dragon to its knees,
And the small heart sparkles amidst the leaves
Of the one thousand flowers, and flares.

Rain Song

My sad-bad rain that falls
In lisp and dibble-dabble
On the porch and under stairs
And puddles in the driveway brimmed
And dolloped by the slow loitering
Of the not-quite clapping hands
So slight they are on primrose
Leaves and the periwinkle
And keeps such babble going through the day.

Cats in beds sleep long
And I, I'd do the same
Or sing
If all the birds weren't gone.
It's silk under the elm leaves
It's slip into the streams
That clasp the globe around,
It's in the stealth to steal
Another tongue than bell
That does not strike but holds
All in its spell
So fresh and so small.

Cracked Looking Glass

The tears, the firebursts and the vows,
The wild caprices and the bouts of pulse
The chills of sieged despairs, those flowers
Bought to match eyes and proffer aphrodisiacs
Of sighs and groans; the seizures.
World at the end of world when dusk falls slow
And all else but a taunting fast and loose.
Smooth skin, shut eyes and gliding limbs.

Love, I note you, stroke by stroke,
And show you how you play with shameless art
In the cracked looking glass that I hold up
What practice has made perfect, if it has.
The fits and starts, the going then to stay
The word, the gesture meant to take the heart
(If it be studied or be not)
Grand ceremonials of a play
By which we tried to live a passion out
By every nuance in a little room.
And cloistered so, tell out our stories
To pass the time until the moon rode high,
Improve upon the life we led,
Give gifts of praise, and so we did.
And if you postured in the looking glass
I made it for you, I held the witchery up
For you to see the secret life I guessed,
That more than improbable, celestial otherness.
And if you acted what I taught
Even as I learned it at your eyes
And your each ruse took on as if we borrowed
From every trick known to the over-wrought
And half-Platonic specialist,
We did it under moon craft or in twilight,

In all the half hours when the world becomes
All that imagination ever hoped it was.

My tear-quenched cost, I number half the ways
We chose a smoky vapor over fire
And tried to make a greater truth
Than what our contradictions could allow,
Exclaiming, as we breathed,
The true irrational.
And yet we were what we are.
And though the smoke is gone there is some fire
In saying so.

We made a play but not a discipline.
Love is the sternest master of the school.
But players tell a truth they cannot know.
They do not live it either, they enact
The fiery powers of instants in a light
Held up to them they cannot clarify.
Cease and be still. The pain is otherwise.
It's in the breaking face the clouds give to the moon
And in the flower that leans upon the air
Pouring its full life out into its scent.

Bleecker Street

Two infants vis-à-vis
Laughing, striking softly out
At one another in their carriage,
The American flag set out in bulbs—
The crookt stars and tawdry stripes,
Aren't they bizarre
To advertise a church bazaar
By backs of Spanish melons?
That child in the butcher shop
With lids so fine-cut over such a blue—
Inviolate—
Out of where?
O pure and neat, severe
Sentinel angel!
Life! Sister! A kitten sleeping
Ready to paw out if I scratch behind his ear!
I'm laden with your bread, your milk,
I'm thinking of you just the way
I'd think of lips, hair . . .
I'd sense like a kiss upon the cheek
The way you seem to be upon the air
Like one come from far
To favor us with careless smiles and blinks
Inscrutable!
But where the lamb hangs in his wool
I meet the waiter taking dinner
To my blind old neighbor,
Sick, blind, alone.
Yes, but we're disabled
To meet the many that you are,
You'd stifle us in backrooms of the soul!
There's no strutting we can do
Like my other neighbor's pigeons who've brought down
Some straw of snatched-up sunlight in their beaks.

Nothing that you do not contradict,
Our gentle, murderous Enigma!
And night comes round the corner after you. . . .

Suite

Afterwards (July 15, 1964)

Debts writing me letters,
Mice running under my bed,
My mother's horse looks in the door,
Her fingers waltz the window pane.

O that piano in the Alps.
Louder it swells, again, again!
I wake. The moon is shining in.
Its stains are on the floor, a chair.
The smashed white clock she cannot mend again.

Nota Bene

I'll break your heart, A. said to me
You'll break my heart, I said to B.
Both did, and still, is my ticker all that smashed?
We get over old wounds by acquiring new ones,
Said C. And thus I obtained all three.

Your Words

Your words cross back from days
I try to think just when it was
You said that beautiful thing
Or chiseled that flamboyant phrase

And thinking am half lost
In pursuit again
Of how it was you looked
When your painted speeches shook
My reluctant heart.

The Beginning

You
Came drifting up to me
As a cat will seek a new home
When a summer master's left.
And I was charmed by that,
I did not ponder riddles, I esteemed
The surfaced play, the light
Inconsequential thing
And wished to be a matchfire for a moth.

And the Platonic Order

And the Platonic order of the morning, chaste,
Spontaneous, with a hot cool sun
The satin cups of the crocus, the hyacinth
Not Greek, not "ensanguined with woe,"
Already the loose knot of violets
Lead me. And I cannot go.

Again, Again

Always that old language for the new:
How many eyes are black or brown or blue.
How many have come naked into bed
The curtains drawn; late morning that lets in
Just so much light to gild the rose-gold head.
That amorini look—intent and bent
To fast desire on nothing else but it
A century long.
How many times. How many arms
How many kisses that the gamblers gave
Or pitched all on to win
Or gaining win to lose again.
How many times. And now you come.
Have cigarettes, cigars, guitars and rum!
How many times! Yet none but this—
So sighing lovers sigh in their excess
To have the heart unlettered in its breast,
Unlettered of all histories but this,
This last be first and none but this!

The Flux of Autumn

All is a golden burst, the wind burning
The golden trees that plunge
Headmost into the burning light and make
A sound as fierce as waterfalls—
Excitable air of dying changes,
Autumn of the year and of the height!

So I by shady walking saw old leaves
Whirled in hardy rings and circles plunged,
Gyration of the fire-plagued spirits crying!
And saw it was a fight to the death this year,
The fortress mountains thinning their own shapes,
Advancing now from thickets of the sense,
From wayward, tall, exultant, sap-choked green,
A hardy brambled green that founders us,
Into this umbre, somber, earth-dark thing
That then at twilight imitates a blue
And in a link, a series, and a bare earth-warded
Chain sets up the gaunter distances
Between their star-reefed differences and us.

What is this dream we make with leaf-rained earth
Or do we live upon a fire not ours
Like absentees of will, Undines of fantasies
Waiting and listening in a rich suspense
Expecting half our dreams to be its selves
And all of what we love our own?
So then the reddening apple is as much germane
And those tuft-headed grasses of the field
Rising above their lower-lying kin
And how they are is how they stand
Leaning upon the wind that moves the mind
To lean upon the same all-mothering stuff
And draw the intricate world more close

Until we'd think the rudest empire of tough chaff and rock
The very form of our subjective wish
Reshaped again within the restless eye
That takes its bearings from the true itself
To enter then on changes of its being,
A changeless changing, transformings into
An ethereal storming, freshening, continuous,

For I have heard those voices rough
As shaggy earth and humming with the earth's own tilth
Or mad as water hurled against a stone
So now you remnant butterfly whose motion makes
A silent music, repeat, repeat,
And you thin clouds who deepen in the skies
Your soundlessness against the surged uproar
Until the four winds seem to swell one tone
From out the banter between field and wood
To let us think all things are full of gods.

As shadow falls upon a rock.
The shadow of a bird has crossed my heart
That we are these, these living things, enough!
By them we make a burning territory
Wherein there walk those influences of sky
At that long moment of the eye
When all leaps upward at some ancient wind
Blown from the corners of some leaf-blocked road
We walk upon in sober truth. To be so caught
By all this phantomed streaming forth
It seems a greater phantom is at work.

Quick-shading now, the battle of leaves,
The airy-quick, a gusty lunging, throbbing,
Metallic clangor, pipes, the errant horn.
Misled by fevers then, by ditches lost,

By fireweed and the hawks that plunge,
This that I'm in's become a changeling cloud.
The clarity of mountains is obscured
By what we'd fortify that must be dreamed.
Old territory mapped and walked
Nightly, daily, in the impetuous eye
Of thought.
                    Until the dream's walked out.

Chartres and
Prose Poems

(1970)

Shore

Running through the thick wiry grasses to the pond where the wild swans nest, by the broad low spit of sand, by the stream pulsing from it, a narrow thing that goes to the sea, by the mossed flanks of the rocks, by the dunes of the pure bright grass, a Holland green.

Running in the soft swift wind, enough to belly out every sail, that rifts the shallow stream with fast lapping waves and drives the cry of a bird against us, one of those stilt-legged, striped-of-wing birds, sanderling or sandpiper, dipping and veering sideways and windward.

Running in the cry of the bird as we come to the pond, agitated too, veined down the middle, ribbed and splintered by the wind's soft blowing. Black the pond, soot black the claws of the firs and roofs and chimney stacks bulky and hairy with vines, all furred black, lampblack, inkwork black, etched and pressed against this western sky of the hue of geranium, a clear still storm of it as the sandpiper soars up shortly to veer and glide over and some troubled other gives cry and counter cry to the first lamentings.

In this light and this like-weeping as we run on now, over the sand that in wet places keeps the reflection of the new hung moon, over the tusked camel hump of the brindled rock whose ridged sides slope to the sea, by pockets of the sea rose, pickets of grass, soft kerchiefs of the grass-sown sand to the wrinkled prairie of waves caught now in the single chord of burning.

Country Villa

What was it like, that country house? You never knew at
all. Long and yellow with a faded coat of arms. . . . A road under ilex
led up to it but this was only walked now, never driven. The ilex was
old, the trunks richly mossed and twisting, perfect for a child to climb
and there were many children, and many did, the boughs permitted to
meet and tangle overhead so that you walked under an almost tightly
woven roof of leaves that gave out scent, an indefinable, dusky scent,
somewhat bitter, somewhat tonic, mixed as it was with the scent of
the brooding family of cypresses toward which the longly shaded
pathway led. It was steeply uphill and small stones rolled under your
feet. On a hot late afternoon you were inclined to go slowly. Never-
theless it was delicious to be toiling under those shadows through
which the sunlight broke, into which the free winds rarely penetrated,
so dense the leaf enclosure. You might be in a latticed tunnel and
when you looked down from the house itself the road appeared to
be no more than a square-cut aperture, a low stooped door that
gave onto the road through much sweet cluster. Yet close-set as the
twisted and moss-painted low trunks were, you might at times break
through and there lay the outside world of a big field gone over to
the blue flowered lucerne. Fields folded into fields, all sloping down
to the road where fields on the other side rode up, planted with rows
of vines that in the early spring looked like rows of green seams or
with haystacks set in what seemed to be mathematically calculated
distances.

Coming out of the shaded pathway you met a haystack here
also, a broad low cushioned thing not unlike an excessively large di-
van. The children had put small Sienese banners in its prickly sides
and the colors drooped on the windless afternoon like dispirited sig-
nals from a battlement.

Beheld in Naples

And following the poor dead child, the ragazza, lying in
a lean brown deal coffin, and it is so lean and brown in the volute
carriage of scrolls and king's crowns shaped like a white valentine,
and six black horses wearing six white plumes that look like feather
dusters taking the measured horsely tread—o slow march tread—that
the file of mourners may keep step with, women and children first—
the sweatered mother—down a side street flowing and flying with
laundry, with balconies hung too with sheets and bedspreads so that
the child rides as in a triumphal procession under ensigns of table-
cloths and banners of slips and shirts past tubs filled with snails and
sea urchins and stands piled with oranges and artichokes, past women
at the stands bowing their heads or making the sign of the cross,
past men with their hats pressed against their chests and fish on fern
leaves and cats underfoot. And at a sharp turning the three strings
of horses halted and a boy running to lead out the first pair under a
rough ancient arch and so into a piazza with two churches and then
into the Corso that leads to the Stazione and the horses halted again.
And their plumes that had tossed taken off and the cars that had been
crawling behind, laden with wreaths of white roses and sheafs of calla
lilies, dashing forward, and the band of mourners gone into the cars
and the horses starting up at a fast clip. And it is over. The child is
really being taken away. No help for it. Follows the descent into the
vast quiet earth.

Studies for an Actress
and Other Poems

(1973)

The Grand Canyon

Where is the restaurant cat?
I am lonely under the fluorescent light
as a cook waddles in her smoky region visible through an open arch
and someone is pounding, pounding
whatever it is that is being pounded
and a waitress cracks with the cowboys lined up at the counter
lumberjacked, weathered and bony
intimates, I would guess, of the Canyon,
like the raven that flies, scouting above it,
of the hooked face and the almost flat sleek wings.

Where is my cat? I am lonely,
knocked out, stunned-sleepy,
knocked out by the terraced massed faces
of the brute Sublime,
color inflamed,
when I came to the edge and looked over:
violaceous, vermilion
great frontal reefs, buttes,
cliffs of rufous and ocher angles,
promontories, projections, jutments, outjuttings
and gnarled mirlitons, so it seemed,
twisting up out of depth beyond depth
gnarled like the juniper tree
rachitic with wind I hung on to
as the raven's wing, glassy in the light of its black,
slid over me

there at the edge of this maw, gash
deepest in the world that a river has made
through an upwarp in the earth's crust,
thickets of tens of thousands of gorges eaten out
by freezing and thawing, tempests, waterspouts,
squalls and falls of the river
with its boulders, pebbles, silt and sand sawing down

127

through the great cake of geologic time,
eight layers laid bare,
the total effect creating what geometrical effect
in a rocky silence so clear
a bird's voice, even a boy's
is spunged out, sucked up by this stillness
stinging, overpowering the ear,
pure condition of the original echoing soundlessness
this voluminous wrung resonance
welling up out of the handiwork
of the demiurge wrestling down there
in an infinity of imperceptible events
some ten million years,

ages blanching to think of,
taking the switchback trail,
slipping and sliding,
forever slantwise descending
into new confrontations of parapets,
chimneys, mantels, segments of angles,
modelings of rock of slacknesses and accidental tensions
combined with the effects of its weight—
the total effect never total for never can you see it all, not even guess
at mazes of the proliferation,
and the river will not be visible
except from a driven angle,
the snaken twists of its rapids looking petrified, frozen
from the distance of a deep mile:

somebody saying a mountain could be plucked up by its roots
and dropped head-first down there and it wouldn't dam up the river
so that the waters would run over

and that the Washington Monument could be kept out of the rain
under one overhanging of an otherwise vertical red wall

where the gold of the light on that chaos of creases nervously darts
like the violet-green swallow stitching its leaps and arcs
over the gliding raven,

over the camber of columns, tawny rotundas of ruins
writhed, mottled, crested with shells,
escarpments
downbeaten by frost and rain,
parallel rangings of
rostrums, pulpits and lecterns,
and the mad Tiberius arches groining
cave holes on cave holes in the same wall of limestone, red
from the ironstone drippings,

Aztec pyramidal temples rising in hundreds of steps
to the summit of the seemed shrine
curtained, girdled with snakes and necklaces of hearts,
wet with sacrificial blood,

rusticated building blocks jutting out in warlike ramifications of forts,
stockades of black frosted rock,
towers of the baldness mounting like obelisks,
pyramidal forms from the sands of Egypt,
crags vertiginous, cupolas, alcoves,
amphitheatres, arenas, organ pipes, flutings,
porches of rock, wedges of shadow in perforated rock,

and the gold of the light nervously darting
on the Bright Angel shale, pink with long stripes,
on the lavender blue of the Shinumo Quartzite,
on the deeper rose of the Hakatai shale,
on the blond Coconino sandstone
riddled, it's said, with the trails of sea worms,
on the grey Kaibab limestone
with casts of shark teeth and horn coral imbedded

like the Hermit shale of the topmost formation
with footprints of salamanders, insect wings four inches in length
and even a dimple left by a raindrop during some era of burning
and hailstorm, torrent and drought,
era on era stacked here,
untold era on era,
as the eye like a long-legged insect on a windowpane
slithers and shudders up and down
the banded and ribboned, ribbed systems of rock,
into and out of shadows,
chromatic world of what glitters like phantoms,
corrugations of scaffoldings appointing to chill
over the continuous surface,
assemblies of aggregations
sand-pocked and pitted,
ridged, wind-serrated,
tawny thresholds in the lying out there of the steeps,
in the drinking up of the stillness
pressed in by the gorged rock
deepening in the light of the motes of beams
under those clouds that like water lilies
enclose within them this silence received
that they graze upon and are gone.

Movie Actors Scribbling Letters
Very Fast in Crucial Scenes

The velocity with which they write—
Don't you know it? It's from the heart!
They are acting the whole part out.
Love! has taken them up—
Like writing to god in the night.
Meet me! I'm dying! Come at once!
The crisis is on them, the shock
Drives from the nerve to the pen,
Pours from the blood into ink.

"Why the Heart Has Dreams
Is Why the Mind Goes Mad"

(After seeing *The Seagull* once again)

The scent of weak lilac, cheap caporal,
The wind in the trees and the dog howling
And K loving N who loves T who loves A—
It was under those cloudbanks there
Under their weight, to meet them
The boy in a fever of grief
So shabby and rash and green
And she so imponderably of the mien
Of the tirading queen.
The boy is all wrung, unstrung,
For his mother has laughed at the wrong time.
Were he other than he, he would leave,
But the truth of her laughter is, and he knows it,
She laughs for no simple reason
And it is this rocking back and forth—
O it is not coldness that seems like shyness,
It is all vivid posturing,
Vain, reckless and melting,
Her dragonfly waist in silk,
Her tinderbox storms, flaring up
With insult worse than rebuke,
Every old hand-me-down flung down
To reduce him from fever to shame,
Weathercock fits that mutilate,
Exhilarate,
Binding the bonds more tight,
For in the next instant she veers,
Is in caressing tears,
Till crumpled at last he is brought to his knees,
To the child he was, his milky mother
So cruel to be kind whose glancing hands
Are like the touches of the willow.

Then goes—to fling himself at the piano—
A melancholy waltz
Heard all over the house—
To which they simply say as if he were the dog that howls
On moonstruck nights—
"Kostya is sad,"
Living so much in the middle of human nature
They cannot be bothered to account for its wildness.

O varied and troubling rhythm!
He knows and knows no better
That clue to the tears she can shake him down to,
Treading on all his prides
So obscurely linked to his fears.
How can he solve himself!
How can he leave this house
Rotten as cheese, a parlor for spiders,
Caught in the netting himself,
How can he manage this knotted pain
Like a retarded, retarding thing,
Himself at breakneck speed of remorse—
Foam caught from the moon
Foaming out over the keys.

O varied and troubling rhythm!
He plays in the house of aging childhood
Known to the draughty parlor,
To the flags of every dream.

Known to the woods, the lake,
The meadow where the crane still walks,
Known to the stage in the garden
Where the curtain flaps in the wind.
Known to the hour of the doleful dog,

To the mauve hour of the handsome man—
Perfumes that accost the quick-flushed cheek—
Known to candors, impulse
To what teased fancy most
Until the feelings, delicate feelings,
Are worn off.
Known to neglect and guilelessness,
Guilelessness, witlessness!
Nina, love, that smashed thing,
Nina, phantomed away,
Her candors of the stuff
To those whose feelings, delicate feelings—
Nina, wandering-witted, astray,
The varied, troubling wind
Beating, beating at the door
Until she is swept in
Like some bewildered seabird she has learned
In imitation of to become,
And he going out of the room
Really to shoot himself this time.

And you see how in the interests of truth,
The anonymous truth that respects no one,
Whether it was intended or not,
His purpose in life was to be broken.

The Smoke Shop Owner's Daughter

The illness had wanted to kill her
Although it had not, quite.
It had left her, however, knotted and pale,
Of the size of a twelve-year-old child,
An underground child, mushroom white,
With pitted cheeks and the look
Of the one for whom it is perhaps too late
To grow up, and so who stands
Somewhere off at the start
Of the about to be and the never not.
And always silent. But then—
Speech was a thing far apart.
How could she say. It had been so long
She had been kept inside and away—
Like a child with a pointed head
Kept in bed in the slanting light
In a place cut off where they store old things,
Like a mad prince of the counterpanes—
Except that it was not so rank,
So slanting and dusty in the weak light,
Though with the dog and the cat it was cramped
At the back of the store (with her mother out front)
In the faint greys that had stayed so long
They came as close to her as a friend,
Close as the sickness, and when they went
Took what she had which was them,
Nothing more, and left her to find her way back.

You saw it there in her eyes.
Something sat there like a small thing
That having been taken away so far
Can't hear the echoes from the near
And does not know how to be
With the strange untrue of the real,
There being, neither, no one to say

If it's that or not or to try
However they might to draw her away
From the tense where she lives of the still,
No one to mend her, baffled and cropt.

After Reading "The Country of the Pointed Firs"

She was the one who lived up country
Half in the woods on a rain-washed road
With a well not near and a barn too far
And the fields ledgy and full of stones
That the crows cawed over and liked to walk in
And the hill and the hollow thick with fern
And in the swamp the cattails and rushes.

It was next to living in a town of birds
But she had hens and a row of bee hives.
When her mother died, and her girl, and Joel,
She told the bees so they'd not fly away
And hung black flags on the doors of the hives
Though they'd always go when they could to the woods
Or swarm on Sunday when she was at meeting.
For each who went she had told the bees.

Change and loss was what the brook cried
That she heard in the night—but she kept snug
With crow-wood for kindling, and the sun shone good
Through the tops of the pines, and her plants
Didn't fail her, and the rosebush always bloomed
By the gnawed fencepost—what the horse had done
When they had a horse and a cow and a dog.

O there had been many, and now was there none?
Lost at sea, they said, her son gone to sea
Lost at sea they said. But if he wasn't
And if he'd come back—so she'd stay till he came
Or whether or not.
Change and loss was what the brook cried
That she heard in the night when the clock whirred.

But when the fog from the southbank came through the firs
Till the air was like something made of cobwebs,

Thin as a cobweb, helpless as shadows
Swept here and there as the sea gulls mewed,
O then it seemed it was all one day
And no one gone and no one crossed over
Or when the rain gurgled in the eave spout
Or the wind walked on the roof like a boy.

Change and loss was what the brook cried
That she heard in the night when the clock whirred
Just before it clanged out its twelve heavy strokes
In the thick of the stillness, black as a crow,
But no scritching now with a scrawny great crackling,
And the rain not trickling, nothing to hark to,
Not even the tree at the north chamber window.

Till she routed it, horse and foot,
Thinking of walking to town through pastures
When the wood thrushes wept their notes
And the moss was thick on the cobbled stones
With the heron wading among the hummocks
Of the pursy meadow that went down to the sea.

And she had knitting and folks to visit,
Preserves to make, and cream tartar biscuit,
She knew where was elocamp, coltsfoot, lobelia,
And she'd make a good mess up for all as could use it,
And go to the well and let down the bucket
And see the sky there and herself in it
As the wind threw itself about in the bushes and shouted
And another day fresh as a cedar started.

In Memory

Josephine Herbst
1897–1969

You believed in a world that has never come
With or without hope of this one
And therefore you would say
"I believe in what I do not see"
Insurgently or laughingly
And walked through parts of your storm
With angels of the enfranchised one
That had been truly born,
Turning the mocking cheek also:
"Who's interested now in / 'Ah, wretched soul!' "
Who, indeed, in a new world
Where the heart might pulse
Fresh, disinterested at last
For everything outside itself
But where, indeed, was that,
Contradictory dissenter?
And who more full of nature,
Broad, human nature,
Who more indwelling
Than you or that loud poet
Out in the fields of feeling?
Nothing was trivial for you
Nor the angular barn in the meadow
At the foot of the broken stones.

Many selves to yourself as to others,
You did not doubt that you were beloved
And by good strangers, friends to you
Bearing the promised language.
Yet skeptic you could doubt
Out of a full heart
Who tried to beat the game

And did so, again, again,
And raised us leaves of hope by that
For something simple like a natural thing,
For something large, essential, driving hard
Against the stupors of too much gone wrong,
And by your intensity
Of flame against the dark
(You beat up flame,
You beat it up against the dark)

Gave us greater want
To change the heart to change the life
Changing our lives in the light that is changing
But which has no future, no yesterday.
O green vine on a pole,
Wanting all mingled with your own deep root,
At home with the alive as wheat,
You would have it that we may break out of ourselves,
The solitude breaking down also.
"We are now men among men, we have brothers"
Was not what you would have quoted
But knew.

In the long nights of your dreams
You were Ondine one time, you were also he
Who was hauled around the walls of Troy.
Inside was a you that lived in connections
Belonging to a thousand persons.
Putting on them, was that how you learned
What you really wore,
Which was joyful wounds, as a poet said?

Were you trusting? You did not expect to be harmed?
In the twelfth hour did you believe and hope for us all?

In the dark, what words, what signs?
Blue air of childhood, did it descend to you?

From your trials how could we not think
You would not come out alive?
Had we not seen you battle before?
And we, swept away
Almost before the door
At which loud haste knocked long,
Believed that this could be
And, too, because you'd have it so
The while a mystery
Burned its way through you.
You did not win and yet
It deeper more deeply burns
Although the seal is on the door,
Although the words go into stone.

For J.

I think of that grave woman in the dark
There by the delicate stream at the pitch of moon,
Valor encompassed by the rare serene.
Difficult life has battered her and yet
With what magnificent strength she outstands that
No matter that the earth be dark and worn.
Might I learn, wasted and much torn,
From whence she gets the laughter of her kind.
Giving and blessing, it enkindles mind
And on the heart its wisdom without rancor fiery-earned
Bestows such light that all seems round
And brought to full, like our redemptive moon.

Requiem

In the sudden white silence, where are you? It seems I carry a letter to you, but the mouth of the mailbox is choked with snow and the box billows, swollen to twice its size by the thick coating of so many flakes already fallen for hours.

I think then to telephone you, seeing a booth, its panes pasted over and opaque like a half-marbled sentry box. But the floor is so deep in snow that I cannot pull the door to. Even the books are thick in it and the mouthpiece is sifted over.

Balked, I walk into the park of the trees of this new foliage, false orchard bewildering like a fruitless spring. From afar strikes one bell practising to be heard.

Is it you calling?

No. Only my heart tolling.

The Giralda

(A colossal statue symbolizing faith that is so adjusted
as to turn easily in the wind. It surmounts the square tower,
formerly a minaret, of the cathedral of Seville)

This was all my light that while
I burned for it in a spiral
And was burned out. Then lit again
And even when burnt out, smoldering.
Think of the girasol, I spun
As even the giralda around my sun.

Faith regards its dominion of rooftiles
(O my fire burnt low).
Faith this weather vane surveying her legends
The buckled roof spanning the vaultings
The turrets of gargoyles.

Faith this dervish turned by the winds
This way and that but fixed to its spire
(O my fire, my faith turns slow)
Though handed by winds every which way.

To the north the mountains to the east the tombs
To the south the thickets of the thorn
To the west the moon that stands straight up
From the leaves of the tree of childhood.

Has the wind forgotten my weather vane
That moaned when it creaked and blew?
O my fire, it does not turn.
Something has gone down.

Song in Sligo

I had a bear that danced,
A monkey on a stick,
A dog that begged,
A cat that moused,
And, slouching by a ditch,
A rook in black of silk.
I had those birds that rode
Upon the levels of the cove
At late long twilight in the north
When the brand of sun still burned
Above the shoddy bridges of the Garavogue.
I had a boat that beat
Up levels of the reed-flagged shore
And rock-grained, rack-ruined battlements.
I had a boat and traveled with the birds
That flew against me in the breath of winds,
To each bend of the river its own mews
Of samite-backed and sable-legged young swans
Who winter from the Bay of Rosses here.
I had an island for my own one want,
A ring of prophecy and scent,
Where trees were sloped upon a moss of turf,
One ruined wall that I could sit against
And dip a ragged net to catch a fish
Of rainbowed armor in the scales of night.
I had a love who spoke to me of wars.
It was the summer of the fires.
Blackout by desolating energy.
You silken tatters of the sliding flow,
I had your voices and your leafy pools,
I have these poisons we must choose.

Grenoble Café

At breakfast they are sober, subdued.
It is early. They have not much to say
Or with declamations fit only for whisper
Keep under pressure the steam of their joy.
She listens, usually. It is he who talks,
Surrounding her with the furious smoke
Of his looking that simply feeds,
Perhaps, her slightly traveling-away dreams
That, if you judge from her cheek,
Young and incomparably unbroken,
Are rich with the unknowing knowing
Of what he has said the time before
And with the smiles coming down the corridor
Of how it will be for year on year,
Nights as they'll be in his rough arms.

Song for "Buvez les Vins du Postillon"—Advt.

In the Rue Monsieur le Prince
That Stephen once walked in hunger and toothache
We drank the wines of the postilion.
O I had a broken tooth myself,
I had broken my glasses as well,
And you, you had lost half your time
In the crooked streets of Spain,
But we drank the wines of the postilion.
O it was lovely at the buvette
In the time of the lilac and cherry
Not to think of the Hotel du Départ
But be drunk on the wines of the postilion
And lovely at the buvette
When a man came by in a blue smock
With a mandolin he did not play,
Yet the lilacs shook in the wake
Of the possibilities of sentiment
Of this marvelous-bodied instrument
Hung with ribbons—so svelte!
O it was lovely at the buvette
Not to think of the Hotel du Départ
Nor weep for lost causes nor why
First you must go, then I,
And O lovely to stay
In the time of the lilac and cherry
And be drunk on the wines of the postilion.

Beaucaire

It was when I was walking I came upon
A chateau, they said, of cigales
No more now than a fort of flowers
To a degree occupied by as much armies
Of plumy grasses as poppies
And bannerets of a pink-headed shrub.
How I found it was up a staircase of weeds
A limping guardian led me to
Through a gate that closed at six o'clock
(When he would show me out.)
Where they were it was dry, one was forbidden to smoke,
There were pine trees and beds of thick iris
And then the yellow ruined face itself
By a remnant wall and a tower case.
When I really arrived they were thundering,
I was abashed as if I were deafened.
There were not only sawmills in the plane trees
And tympani and assemblies of cymbals
But sometimes whole wheezing and rustling
Harpsichord companies.
Earth throbbed with the sound
As if there spoke from its roots
A thousand acres of the parched grass
And air echoing, echoing,
And distance itself aching.

Climbing the spiny stair
Of the slot-eyed tower
I saw in scantling air
Names dug deep into its walls
And place or date to make it clear
How long they wasted here:
Blancpain in fifteen ten,
In seventeen twenty Lebrun,

Vertaud, when Richelieu's cannon was loud
That did not bring these great stones down,
And Luca, who did not record the year
He carved his name for Gabrielle
In day-long dark on afternoons
Perhaps as hoarse with wild, gay din.

To Speak of My Influences

To speak of my influences:
Above all, your eyes,
And next, that jar of the bell
When I think it is you who call.
Since half the time it is not,
I have fevers to quell.
To speak as well
Of the rain in the night
We suddenly heard lying there,
That satin'd stress of a crazy wine
Silverly beating down.
That music, too, you played—
Or was it your élan,
Dense and rich? A sea-clashed mist
Warred with the wracked pulse
That danced my blood to flame
Plagued by certain notes
Of irritable brilliance and flutes
Velvet-mouthed. Ah, monotone
Of phrases faded into dissolution!
Dazed, credulous, I lived
Unbalanced by such powers
As ruled me like that speech you played
And rain's metallic waterfalls.
They ruled me, yes. Eyes kissed by eyes
And ears stunned by the delicacy
Of that fire-in-the-straw art
Wished no more than to be
Set once more alight.

To speak of my influences:
By force of fate, you said,
Who came with masks, imported more
When the suave cords were twanged,
Increased the speed at which it wound

Its flaunting silk of sound.
O heresy! All changes
Save this art at which we play,
The instant, drenched in rain,
We imitated once again
But have we the cunning to
Keep enthrallment vined?

Straw-in-the-fire love,
It's no morality play we're in,
Nor can we trick time
Nor end where we began.
Let us end as we will
While I make apostrophes
That will not more excel
Than your eyes, our dance,
And we'll love on by chance.

A Civilization Constantly Worrying About Itself As It Goes
On Doing What It Is Worrying About That It Is Doing

Something is definitely *not*.
Those vices must I cultivate
Simply in order to find out
The occasion for this violent non-grief?
Am I being infected by air?
By the perpetual warnings of committees
That we are rushing swine-like like lemmings
Head on down the rocks to you-know-what
Which cannot be stopped because interest and profit
Always act too late?
But I wouldn't know, I merely live
On what I lived. Who's swimming
In my Lake Success?
How am I calling the shots for faith?
"Grand strategists are usually bad chess players,"
The shade of a woods is one thing,
The income from it another,
And their world is tomorrow
We despoil today.
Idols succeed public idols.
Once it was Marilyn, now it's—you name her.
Once Yevtushenko, now Voznesensky,
And the ugly is foremost the master,
Allaying a vertigo it escalates
With Muzak.
May only the ugly drive out the ugly?
Or are we just celebrating our sumps and our drains
Before we fall into them?
Well, cheers, old cock,
It's over my head, I'm out of my depth
And frankly right now out of my world
In a world who possibly wants
Except the mixmasters?

(Take my hand, darling,
Be not what I prey on
That preys on me, or . . .)

Lead in the Water

Lead in the water, mercury in the air.
Too late! I hear that phrase my old love made
That taunted and that sombred and that died
On bell waves that still rock this boat,
This head. We work against such menace
Of far thunder. Each night we hear the birds,
The elephants, we see the birds all slicked
In oil, the elephants uprooting trees for water
And thousands, count them, will be shot.
Lead in the air and mercury in water . . .
Our Second Revolution's brought us this.
Those children first who worked sixteen hours a day
For their own good, so cotton capitalists said.
Ours now, we thrash in, made fat-headed
By computers, the huge and stunting. And who said:
"Over-population, over-organization"?
By this or not we lessen and we lust
The more for moon-landings, a way of death.
Escape artists, fed on swill,
Wanting more and more, forever more.
Not one "improvement" will we let go by,
Still cuddling picture postcards of the ideal,
Our hamstrung set, our soiled state
Led by the automated hypocrite. Years like this
Of miles on square miles of the mangrove acres
Of dense-leafed forests as leafless now
As if an atom bomb had cleaned them down to stone.
But who will judge the victor? Might's still right
In this our swollen pigsfoot of a state.

"For Such a Bird He Had No Convenient Cage"

Her dreameries had been raided.
To the utmost rag and bone they had been hauled
Over the coals and up the flagpole for inspection,
To their limits they had been exposed
And all but sneeringly investigated.
Therefore what to do?
Invasions like this are of a classic port,
Our histories tell them to the last redoubt
Of unjustified sacking and not one stone left.
Hers was not of the same case.
It was not Oven Cleaner against Mace
And massed blue faces, snipers invisibly
Picking off your poor Jack, the place so broad
Hostilities had everywhere to hide.
It was not the roving muggers and armed bands,
The keeping up of nerve which means increase
Of the not-thinking or—odorous consequence
From all the crooked coldness, emptiness
That slacks the purpose in a waste of war.
It was less erect and more elect than that.
It was friends retreating into wordlessness,
Hauling in their sails, as one might say,
Like love going back on what it'd said and sworn,
Though that would numb and numb to the bone.
It was the pain of others beginning to show through,
It was *angst* about their almost inhuman bravery,
It was hearing the wound gnaw in them,
Phagocytes at the stormed body.

Resistance Meeting: Boston Common

It is Spring in the Common.
We are among friends.
The smog of confusion has lifted.
Now may light shimmer from the tree,
Now we need not go mad on abstractions
about Power, Fire Power, Garrison, Arsenal
Fire Power, Power, Poseidons
(giving a "multiple warhead Navy Missile" the name of a god)!

Now is Deceit not the General
nor Equivocation the master of tongues
as the firm-voiced speakers speak,
laying it down in a way that is clear,
every word counting, explicitly, sparely,
the clarity being the astonishment,
pricking up the ears, alerting the heart,
though we, incidental among the hundreds at ease all over,
are not the target of aims
nor are we in the toils that have seized whole forests at once.

April in the Public Garden.
The boys who will be drafted are here,
some bearded like disciples,
others with the large dark eyes of *The Volunteers of 1792*
as painted by Thomas Couture,
horsemen-like as a painter might see them,
stilling, instilling their fire
of so much being to be praised by the future.

No point in going on about handsome people
with their thick hair glittering in the wind
about which we have had much comment from ads
so that we are less free to think of Titian's *Man with a Glove*
or a Degas portrait of some olive-skinned pride,

the élan of the painter and subject met at the point of imagination
where the magnificent being
garbed in the full dress of his civilization
completes in himself by his beauty
the rose of every expectancy.

For those lounging and lolling here,
what painter will arrest them in their gear,
at their height of time?
Not hardened yet or tarnished, standing yet
upon the grounds of choice,
still at the moment of decision
or at the moment before decision.

April in the Public Garden.
Also glittering are the hides of the horses
that the policemen sit on like Order and Reason
which is not unlike the order and reason of superior fire power,
the order of Poseidons and nuclear umbrellas,
the talked-about order of seabeds to be used for launching pads

which is not of the order that the speakers are speaking
in spite of the iron order of defense systems (one already obsolete)
dug into mountains so deep it is a whole way of life—could survive
a direct hit for thirty days—

An order it is news to hear of in the open air where public persuaders
usually slide from "fourth class nations" to "regardless of race, creed
    and color"
for the good of the manipulated, card-indexed,
if we are to believe what we read about the faceless ruled by the
    faithless,

An order that has always been known,

known, forgotten, denied
under the pressure not to distinguish what is true from what is
    necessary,
flying the flag of expediency,
which is the mere power of the mind
or the idea, the pure idea of man
witness on his own terms to what he knows,
making and re-making what he is.

Panting dogs run free from their masters,
and when the applause thickens
in the animal excitability of those who have not lost faith
in the light that is mirrored for which all thirst,
or are said to thirst,
join it in a salvo of barks

as the speakers continue to speak of an order
other than the mere boast of the megaton
which is of the stung resolution
of the integrity of being
fully to resist, dissent,
to take the difficult step,
"choosing with all of your lives,"
to bring to bear
energies dispersed in fall on fall.

All this on a bud-gemmed day whose luster
the words of the speakers do not wither,
trying to say the honest thing
about the hard thing to do:
resisting with what doesn't give way
in an hour or a day:
going to war or jail,
hiding in churches or Canada.

April in the Public Garden.
We have heard the message, they have not departed,
for the rain does not fall with the same prickling on us;
it is not we who must weigh
the passive acceptance of a code
against the conscience—or else—
nor shall our blood enamel the pages of the book of some life,
nor are we expected to become heroes (or anti-heroes)
by dispersing the jellied fire
and the chemicals depositing arsenic in the soil.

On Going by Train to White River Junction, Vt.

(The Connection Severed in 1966)

It interferes very little
As it lays down its way.
When it needs to, it follows a river
But does not prevent the roots from their water
Nor by the smut-faced boulder
A small stream from joining a larger,

Nor smashes up hills nor halves them—
Roots and the intricate indwellings thereof
Exposed, and the earth become mud,
Oozing and bleeding away—

Nor removes ledges of sunlight
On cliffed parallels of rock
Nor savages nuances of meadow
Nor rips away mosses in a hollow
Nor requires that sawn woods stand like so many scorched
  matchsticks
Nor musters out ranks of cornstalks
Nor engorges great swatches of dingle
Of ostrich fern in the blue-heroned swamp.

You travel with it and the stones by the river—
By the tussocked meadows
With ponds set glittering like an eye
In the fine lashwork of twigs and boughs in a tangle
Continually nourished so near their mother
By the long runs of sweet water—

Its course neither mathematically severe
Nor of the convenience of martial order.
The scrolls, the cartouche of mists, wisps,
Breathings in crooks and bends

Fume out from a hill undismayed by the disarrays of so much
    unfolding,
Discontinuous flowing

By the green baize of molehills, of ridges,
In pastures the serene flanks of white horses,
Under light that dazes and deifies
Cows winding in among eskers.

Motifs from the Dark Wood

My love was stolen from me,
Carried away like raw youth in a coach
Sang the dying voice of the morning
By a black shed where a bird was caught,
Fluttering and clawing, its eye
Liquid with the glycerine of crying,
Its low warble as it strove webbed-over,
Caught in the threads of that stooped porthole
That gave on the east, sea of cloud,
Where the sanguineous carnation of the late-wintered sun
Reached out to lay its blood
On the blood of the bird,
The dusking webs inflamed by the rays,
Inflamed by the rays as by blood.

Like our childhood troubled in the lost park
At the coming of night on a low-clouded evening
And the slowing down of the rhythms
In the paling of light and the quieting
As the edge of the wood thickens
Into which the vespers of small green voices
Have huskily entered and halted . . .
Coming from meadows at sunset
Seen through the tarlatan of blossom
How slow our walking, our pausing,
Dawdling over the bridges
By water winding through rushes.
Outbursts of voices! A sudden star!

Can we ever not linger, delay . . .
On a pond of moon that lolling sail
May flare us out on a far journey . . .
Rifflings and ebbings, departures . . .

Your hand on mine unsettling me
As music would a tree.

II

The brambled chase in the rides of the forest
As the wind blew its hunting horn.
Following after its notes under leaves,
Through the down-reaching boughs of fir,
Parting our way through them and briar,
Till we came to the twilit avenue
Of trees in ill-set rows
By a brook engorged, gone green and broad,
And the passage of whispers done.

Was it here we dreamed we saw
In a round-centered point like a grove
A spreading-antlered stag and doe
Beside a shaft of stone fenced round
By sparse, rigid iron
And further palisading it
Rivals as of unknown flowers
Blanche-tall but crimson-mouthed.

It was like a chapeled grove
So wan the light come down.
Set deep in moss the name
On this neglected thing.
 Abruptions of a light
 When an eddying wind might bring
 A kind of shudder back . . .

And what begins again,
What begins, who tries to speak

As if through webs upon the mouth,
Who begins, who tries to speak

As if through other lips
Begins to and despairs,
Begins to and cannot.

Moth! What has happened!
You that appear!
O in the wood wept
Drawn on by that fey . . .

Thereafter into the dark
Who has eaten of the bird's heart.
At every seventh step a drop of blood
In the middle of this square of wood.

Moondial

To speak of this hot day: the flaming fields
Filled to the brim with scorch, tasting of singe
And bake and brown: those gasping trees, some dying
At the top: a tangle of long-legged flowers,
Their faces put askew upon their stalks,
And Queen Anne's lace as slant on crooked stems:
Earth ribbed to a near extreme,
Balding of grasses burnt and white with dust,
The lank weed bitten with zest:
Flight, erratic, of the ill-trained grasshopper
And butterflies who test what flowers are left,
Riding them down from prong to prong. . . .
And what with this thin harsh and hacksaw whirr
Of insects that succeed the soft-set song
Gritting and grinding like the shears of time
This last of summer lags
Where cobwebs keep their dusty disrepair
On bushes sere and crackling, juice of leaves
And moist hues gone, all gone,
While on their stalks the flags of leaves hang down
Limp and sapless on the pithless stem
And somewhere else the frazzled leaf has shown
This young tree turned to russet, starved for drink.
Sahara flames
Upon the tracked and rutted, bare-bit ground
Where feet have trod it to a kingdom come.

Into this parched land I come, to the long
Starvation by skies, while in my heart's
A counterpoint—
You know the road so splashed by shade
And then so trodden white where the moon fell in
The dialog made for mild delirium
Not unlike the contagious jubilation
Of these small stringsmen of the grass

Who pluck the long high C.
And then that moon that stared us blind
Or me.
And I would cross by battling stones
Those streams we did of fumy mist,
Against the unremembering surge, to take
The reversed step, and plunge again
Into the vanished silvers without name,
Dazzle of the soft sound of small winds,

And without sanction now to speak that speech
The great night took from us or let us think
We spoke, however wordlessly,
Though you'd but live therein and bask with me
On the lip of the moment, deep brow of the hour.

We walked in moonstuff, lawn and tissue of it,
Past forests chained by it and molded so
That levels of its fountains of dark growth,
Tier upon tier of rich, broad-plated leaves,
Were sculptured by the massy flood,
Fey governor of the insubstantial.
While certain trees, the locust and the walnut,
Were so exposed to all that clarity's balm
Each semi-tropic, half Italianate leaf
Seemed so defined you'd think a draughtsman's pen
Had cut it out of air. Serene, precise
Illumination of the form—
Bleached by light the serrate leaves
On urn-shaping boughs.

And walked we by the harvests of the light,
By meadows where it lay so heaped we might
Have gone to gather it and toss the stuff
And play it out like spray or tuft

Or dip our hands in it to the wrists.
And walked by over-arching boughs, down grass-rimmed roads
Where darkness comes to settle in again
And build its tenebrous structure shade on shade.
A bridge somewhere in middle, made of motes,
Is swaying in the windless air
And as you look again it shifts,
Twinkling and flickering on the still-bound earth.

And then by pastures where it browsed,
Our blameless phantom, till it mixed
With sheep unshepherded and cow,
Heavy-breathing, pulling at dim stalks,
And horses starting up,
Their hooves belling on the drum-hard earth,
Snuffling and tossing out their manes flung dark
Upon the supernatural substance of the light.
And doors in forests leading into doors,
Some bannister of air down that steep hill
Set thick with boles and heavy-hanging leaves,
A snail-shell spiral coiled from out that press
Of traveling loomed and sweet evaporate.
And thus she ascends, descends,
Making her acres everywhere
When from the press of shadows we come out
Into the full untutored dazzle lying bare,
Hills rounded on hills, cobweb sewn.

Myth-making mist and resurrecting light
How still and calm and yet the vapors toil
Up flank and crest to erect their castles there.
Nothing of this will burn us. It is wet.
And yet there glitters up a signal bough
Crusted with diamond dryness or just blanched
Into a great stark bone of flower.

But in the valley such a seethe of foam
You'd think the glitter broke into a song
Too faint, though, for grains of light to carry.
It bore along the nerve and under skin.
We almost could not hear it so we sang.
We were animals of the moon
We stood from out the thatchings of the leaves
In the full gaze as they who would defy
The two-in-one, the life and dying of it.
Its tumult trilled the vein of every thing
And dressed the trees.
Perfect they stood and were the more perfected
We thanked the light for falling as it did
To show their every tangle in the whole
Of wildest, most cross-flowing intricacy.
Such wildness asked for ceremony.
We rose and then we danced a formal tread
Of measure to the trees that graved
Their wilderness upon the thing
Within ourselves that drank it in
We drank the air that drank of moon,
Deceptions that it practised—or were they
Intensifyings of the way things were,
Crazings to the blind who see they see
Or think they do? It flows upon them,
They are washed in curd,
Original essence they say they've fallen on
It is too fair, it bewilders them,
Their senses thrash, they behold, they die
Into one another, into grass, the wanderer airs,
Dying would not ask to be reborn.
There is a moment on the moondial. It has come.

And must the moon thin and the light grow dull
And all that dazzling sunlight of the dark

Be strained through gauze for nothing?
Must the small-eyed spider strike down the wall
For slow murder of a moth,
Fireflies, their lights working on and off,
In fetters of the caught?
And must the dawn wear the world away
Of mystifying touch in twining light
When by a window flows the night
Die to the mind as the light goes out
And the wings open of day and you perceive
A slaughter of innocents—
Some long antennae or a gossamer thigh—
Fragments of the ephemeras.

Mad are the questions that a blindness woke,
A waking up like blindness to all else.
Must I beg to be washed of the moon dust
As I soothe the enfevered flowers of fissured earth?
A bird turning a corner in a wood
A star that glides into and sifts the leaves
A blade of grass that stirred in sleep
To startle us—as if with noise!

I raise again these moon-splashed fields,
Like half-remembered legends I recount
How apparitions skeined us in a coil
Where wholly given, wholly found,
Our beings' threads were wound.
Secessions, then, by sun!
But not from the One.

Attempting to Persuade You to Go for
a Walk in the Public Gardens

It was so pleasurable,
I wanted it to be so free,
I wanted to be talented for life
With the stamina of a rocking horse
Walking with you out of the dust
Of our bookkeeping duties.
The common daylight I wanted
In a company of others under the plantains,
Park-strolling by the pigeons
Of rainbowed necks under the lindens,
Tress lengths of the willow
There by the toy temple,
By the Camperdown elm shaped like a girl,
By the Belgian elm and the oak,
That parasoled "sweetheart tree,"
Its green rind overwrought
By boasting heart on heart.
I wanted it not especial,
The sweetness was in the usual,
Merely the swan boy as he pumps
The bicycle pedals of the boat
That glides at a cortege-like purl
Solemn with children, heaving with mothers,
Merely the civil order of statues—
General Washington on a horse
Apple green, of corded chest,
And Edward Everett Hale about to get
Out of his stone to take a walk—
Under the long-reaching boughs of the beech to be
Disarmed by its knotty intricacy
As two gloved women are
                                who remark
Upon its fine-grained bark.

I wanted what the day was,
The prophet bird, auguries
Cast down by a branch of leaves,
Merely the simple and natural,
The slightly euphoric and free,
Trees named that we might learn
About more kinds than one,
Stone examples of the great
Or at least not insignificant
To remind us of something more
Than our trivialities.
It was the idleness of leaves
Knee-deep from the waftage of other days
Coming into the eyes
And those we met, adrift
On esperances, reveries,
Those worlds locked up in all our heads
Of visages of memories
Particular, unique, unknown,
Yet ancestral as a cloud
We move from, half unknowing
Till a waking sleep is torn.
It was the garden feeling,
It was the Eden good
Here by a lawn of water come
Upon it, to touch us,
Touch us, and let befall,
Stung into fire,
Helpless desire.

Grief Was to Go Out, Away

Grief was to go out, away
From this bedside of cliffs and shells,
Awakings in mornings to white-raged manes
Hoisting themselves up over rocks
And the white mother of foam sped
In a thickened broth curdled white
Back to the throngs of the oncoming rigors.

Grief was just in the having
Of so much heart pulse gone out and away
Into absence and the spent shadow
Of what ran from our fingers as ripples
Of shadow over the sand and what eluded
In a bending of mirrors the tipped tints and reflections
And was just so much running down the packed sands'
Mile-wide blondness of bird-tracked floor.

Was to behold in leaving, as if for the first time,
The fair-weathered crown of the mole
And the light chained to the grass-scattered peak.
Between the gates of the bullet-round rocks
Was to pluck up by the roots the salt hay
Where the seaweed lay wine red
And the foam was combed with gushed red
Was to leave carrying sealed in some envelope

Commandments instructing through leagues down
Where all must be seen through the hidden,
Through shade upon shade, down through layers,
Where all must be seen suspended in the stilled inner scene,
And the word must guard the deed and the inner word
Must not spill its center of smoke
Or break out from the windows of music
Playing deep in the night no one may arrive to

While you come back to your life
In a strange grace of gratitude,
Loving the least and most meagre
Of the held to, the unchosen given,
For here stand the encircling premises
By which don't they leap from, the distances?
And even as in the beat of the running foam
The enhalting power of the thing
Crowding the mind, pouring over the eyes?

Is it in the poignancy of tests
That we strike fire at the source,
At farewell that we clasp what we know,
And as if it were dying, run to embrace
Our life lying out there, misadventured, abstruse,
In the great wedge of light beamed forth—
Like messengers sallying out
To your "I see! I see!" bearing a scroll
On which the word is almost decipherable.

Studies for an Actress

(After having heard Galina Vishnevskaya sing in Dubrovnik)

What she has known, how may our hearts surmise?
Grace that is willful, wit that alerts
Misfortune that it jests with to attract
That she disarms then by a daring step,
Her heart grown richer by this peril met.
And yet a circumstance too small and tight
And she, estranged, cannot invent.
A cloudy counterfeiting takes her up,
Imbroglio of play to which she's card,
The trump they slap, the queen of restless mouth
In that quick living crowding towards the grave.

Yet turn on her the hour she's long rehearsed,
Some knife-edge of the pillaged and profaned,
She pivots on her heel and she is Faith
Like one who stands upon a balcony
Above strange ruins in rooms and streets below
That hordes new loosed like rumors from their masks
Now run upon, more dark than dream,
The which she meets with such a scorn of calm
You'd think she knew a triumph that could come
From something more than malice and than wrong
And this outfacing brings her prisoners—
Lovers who'd have their eyes put out
By such a gathered radiance.

One instant then, and she has veered
When those light things called thoughts
Solidify, grow obdurate as rock.
She flees all action now, she has gone in
Upon a demi-day that sinks towards night
Under instruction from the strangest powers
She would appease and cannot, who reveal

In the most obscure and sinking down of ways
This that they want which will fulfill
This that she does not know, which she must do.
Can she turn back? The path is overgrown.
Ahead,
Roads like lines in the palms of the dead
Now fade.

And must she be who cannot be
This that she scarcely knows she lives
Which baffles in its large, impersonal strength
(Beyond herself and borrowed from the race)
Except that she has guessed it deviously
And it takes over now and glitters out. . . .
We saw her coming, tilted on her heels
Pale her mouth, her body cast aside,
Quick knowledge made it light as any shroud

And eagerness, the rashness of a child,
Envisaging such pleasures as
Riding in a carriage in a fall of flowers
Contracted to that fine formality
That comes upon the soul when it perceives
Just what deceiving passions must take leave.

Is it a play of cross-grained theme
That she would have it that she's acting in
In an unbelievable, intemperate zone
Aloft with figures dwelling in the skies
Big-backed, with arms upraised, in stony robes,
Saluting reverberations in the clouds
Or then—the muted, trembling time
When ailing of her differences or not
She is no more than mere
Dissembling in a mirror?

Soggietto mitologico of this known theme?
Denote her history, if you will, by scenes
If that is how a life can be summed up
Except she believes her differing masks hide no one
But what the action brought to her to be
As if they were a foreign element
That she put on and then put off,
Performing in them alien acts,
The I that was another, that odd she.

And so she thought until the prince of shades
Got into the broad bed where she lay propped.
This was a nuptial scene beyond all doubt
For he would extract from her sleep-bound head
By dense green shadows laced there by a tree
The moon, the stars that grow on boughs,
The moon in her horn drawn by a griffin,
Everything eyed and starred,
Feet bounding like swallows tilting off earth,
The bounding feet of mirth

And then those figures fixed upon a point
Forever at their height and in their hour
When flushed they pierce the dragon's jaw
Or bring the severed head back home,
Who do not change thereafter, tire, nor want
For they are of the fixèd state
Of emblematic figures outside time—
That armored angel on his horse reared back
In wild-eyed excitement—

These crowd the habitations of her sleep
And are not kindly when she wakes,
Garbed figures, rapt and wrought
All to one aim and ending, blazonries

Like constellations of a zodiac
She pulls against and yet is driven by,
And she would ask these players of the immense
Pardon for her fitfulness.

And yet to all this she has come very late
And she forgets, she loses then her place.
We see them at the height of their excess
Who do not change thereafter, tire, nor want
And she is of the shuttling flux
That knows extinction even as it's born,
And she is sightless now with flagging search
That cannot state its end.

A leaf that falls upon a book,
An autumn of a young day come too soon,
And she has lost the thread that let
Those emblems forth, that rich connecting
Between their powers and broad awaking.
Deep knowledge dressed their concentrates.
Then had she moved in such a light of it
As if beneath their very protectorate.
Now, dying bell notes decrescendoing!

And so she falls half out of life,
Out of the net of things into the dark,
Who has no strength now for that bright-in-dark,
That second life those emblemed figures knit.
Blind fit. Nothing to hold her back from this descent
Into a void, opaque, unlit,
When out from feeling, cut the links,
Like torches quenched in sand.
And this is a kind of falling-out she also knows
A kind of hero flails. Which she cannot.
Caught now in her alternatings

Before the incessant intervenings, changings,
And this is twice-known, many-times-more-known
Indifferent death, suggestible on every hand
To light and just as soon converted to the dark.

II

There is a binding element
The which when had, sustains the crazy shifts
Of mind, the turnings and the twistings of the heart,
And those odd twins, the wish and will,
And which, when known, assembles, gathers up
All that will sustain and nourish it.
And is it this that forged the angel's smile,
The gay stone lips, the strong wings folded back,
And is it this of which the poplars speak
Glittering and shouting in the full, strong morning light
And is it this in gaunt cathedrals raised
Of shadows steeped on shadows, mountainous space?

And is it of the mind or heart?
Half human, is it more than that?
And can you give it names like joy, desire,
Like expectation, hope, or triumph known?
Is it of essence alien to the name,
Alien to time, beyond the body's will?
You seek for it, it cannot be invoked. . . .

But if it's lost, the key is lost,
The light is out, all is inert and stony,
What's loved it is not known one loves
Nor is the bird beheld, its stripes denoted,
Its savage black head with the open bill,
Its rosy-russet wings half spread
In battle with another bird
Over a helpless beetle, taken to heart

Nor taken to heart the *festoni* on the *ara,*
The godded bull's horns rising out of ivy,
The true and single government
Of the anthology of forms.

It is of the airiness of apparition
And what has not been founded on a legend?
Great cities had their start in such a light
As when after a battle someone saw
The famous horsemen, half-god brothers,
The famous offspring of the swan-loved Leda,
(The round-eyed ones according to a sculptor)
Watering their horses at a spring.
Until they came there was no spring,
They struck it forth the way they came from air,
Sing there in the Forum on which all turned
To prophesy how Fortune would grow great.

And this she knows and does not know
Assailed by knowledge of a plenitude
The dense, packed world refutes in paining ways.
The world is real, so was the spring that gushed,
So are the rough-cut stones that house what would deny
All that we see. The world is real, and are her falterings real,
And is her weakness truth, her vacillations?
That wending in between the gulfs,
That effort to create the links,
The correspondences how difficult, unfixed,
To set and fix?

And what but the mind sustains the cross-grained theme?
She judges this in that immoderate light
In which the monuments are set.
As to the stones and pillars it gives voice,
Those involutions, that crazed checkerwork

That if it or heart not open out,
Stand in their splendor mute.

She prays now to the smallest thing
Under the black brocade of pines,
She prays for the wind muffled in them,
For the fields in the shimmer of butterflies,
For valerian, dianthus, columbine,
She prays to pray, but cannot start.

Now to the violet light she recommends
When skies open into skies
That clamor of the throng of voices
Kept down, locked in, but murmurous as bees
Ready as ever for the nuptial flight,
Passionate, wholly passionate.

She prays if nothing else to be
In some dissolving medium of light,
A pond that's set to catch the arrowy beams,
Reflective and obedient as that.
She prays then to change
If it's in changing that things find repose.
She prays to praise. She prays to be
Condensed now to one desire
As if it were very life performing her.

Uncollected Poems

Bad Times Song

Where is my cat, my rake,
My poultry seasoning and my stick?
Where is the heart I had who flung your hat
Over the millstream years back?

Where is my tail and purpose strait
For which I fought and won with luck
And where my kin of shining hue
The dark put up?

How do I live and by whose right?
When the war goes on, the price goes up.
Whose treasuries may I sack
And who would give me ransom should I try?

To ask such questions is a childish rote.
Besides, they do not fit
The answers given by the great.
A snake under every stone,

In every suitcase and in every bed,
The thing to do is not to ask but act.

Moralizing Overheard in a Forest

Your duty is to cling,
I heard an old oak say
To its well known and much
Advertised ivy.

I'd have you insinuate
Your charms into every part—
Naturally, I mean of me—
Even underneath

My rugged old bark
And clamber up my trunk
Succinctly to the top.
You have feelers. You must feel,

You have tendrils, cover me.
As I am erect and firm
You must from base to crown
Confirm my grand consistency.

Do not flutter. Simply hang
On to me by every knack
Nature's given you. Art
Is not needed, save

The supple art to do
What Nature, if not I, first taught you.
Nor will you, like the honeysuckle,
Strangle me, I know,

By winding round so tight
I am nearly sapped

Of my liberty to do
With my boughs what I want.

Nor are you venomous
Like that three-leafed thing
That creeps and crawls along the ground
To get its vicious root up

My unresisting slope.
You are healthy. You are not,
Though you cherish me,
Of a gluttonous appetite,

Nor am I simply host, my dear,
To a parasite.
You give beauty, I support.
O darling, how you decorate

My barbarous pole with your crisp coat.
Now assist me in this thought:
That though you cannot bend me
(I am stout)

You're half my gamboling prisoner
I liberate by standing pat.
Is not this a lively pact
And a symbiotic act?

Alas poor lovers who would imitate
The perfect pitch we've reached.
The one may try but is too agile
The other is not staid nor bold enough.

Too great a consciousness untethers
Root of vine and oak.
Who'd get together must lament
Singly and apart

Love as a bad joke.

For an Orchard Tree

For that tree with no fruit but its flower
And that flower the sum of its being
In wind, water, and air
I would like to speak, but who may speak
Of such a pure tree of flower?
Only some strain of song
About to ascend on a line light as vine
May translate this effect of flower
And agitation tranced in a bower.
The rose-dark stem,
The rose-backed flower.
To stand at the midmost of this tree
In the everywhere of its flower . . .

Bees, their wings making diamond light
In that gauze of the wired beat
Of joy elate on its nourishment
Feed there in the furious strength
Of creatures at the pitch of their bent.
To stand under the roof, by the wall of these flowers,
The intercrossed rooftree boughs and light bars
Of boughs making walls
And as the peer bee lives on flower
To live as he does this hour,
Strewn over, the very eye strewn
With the light of the flower and the hum of light
Of the bee's nesting and the bee's rapt drone
In the iridescence of stamens gold-pronged
Tipped by the gold seed from the dark center . . .

Else how to measure this quality out,
How to strain and figure it forth,
How to balance the bee's vibrating of a fantastical wing,
Frame of light thinner than wind,
Against the bough colored the stain of fruit?

Music and paint.
                    Leonardo's study of flowers
Camber of the petaled outfolding
In a fold under fold involuting
To the fringed seed swelling,
You are nearer the soul of the thing.
Flowers so lightly drawn
They dwell like the allegorical one
Half emerged from, half meshed in the mists of the mind.

Standing in air dyed by the sun,
Stamped, printed, designed over,
So many flowers from the wood,
So many petals to a stem
Till the stem is lost to rose skin,
Wood is pure floret, pure burgeonet
Tendrilled and knotted and knobbed
With the foiled deep rose just come
From the vat of the bud, more crimson stained
Than when, betaking of air it has inbreathed
Another hue of its changing—
Rose backed by the support of that which comes
From the wood and's allowed by the bud
To utter its syllable in a tinged cloud
For which, in the slumber of winter,
Hooded in summer, it waits and stands
That for a week in spring
It may expend to the last ounce of its sap
And last strength of the wood root and stem
This birthday of its being—

Ah, standing just here before
Those ones gone over into flower, lying flat on air,
And others in a very twisted downshaft overcome
By the rare burden of flower bent down

God's fire we owe a death to
In that sacrifice of the stem for its flower,
Earth for wood, wood for flower,
Even, at the base of the tree,
A few sprouting there . . .

Doggerel of a Diehard Who Sleeps
in a Nest of Newspapers

Goodbye, old venerable barn
Of apple scent, ladders, web-works,
Hillsides patched and pied,
Mill waters racing, ledged rocks,
Striped dawn, wind in the pulpits of the spring,
Goodbye. And all my pieties thereon.
Goodbye. I'd like to make an epitaph,
I'd like to fit the words right
But I'm disabled, that's a fact,
By being long my own abyss,
Outfitted with the place
If place there is, of this
Pocket-sized mare's nest.
Severings of long ago
Petrified the will by which
The live connectives graft
To carry me up and out.
I've grown of my own depths
The depth itself. That circumstance
That at first we kick against,
Raving of our good intentions
For a New Life,
Becomes at last by some pact
Of suicided want
A natural habitat.

So now, what's the score?
Stopped watches of a life
Is a recurrent metaphor:
Boughs I brought into my room
Cut from the trunk.
They flower that won't have fruit
Who fill my room with light.
No epitaph for that.

The soul's out of joint.
Is failed language the point?
Who made the grinding time-spirit?
This pomp of bombs and cult of what
All agree to be—
O murderous ugliness!—
From you I fled to
Mossed creatures like my barns
And brooks not quite polluted yet.
Properties and props
Going, going, gone,
O stale emptiness!
Life! When was it
That you were!
And those neat engines that convert
The Real into the Ideal!
Who would praise the flowery bough
That had no purpose for its flower
And, cut from its source,
Flowered anyhow?

Index of Titles